GIFTED AND TALENTED TEST PREPARATION

COGAT® GRADE 3

300+ Questions /
2 Full-Length Practice Tests
Level 9

Savant Test Prep™
www.SavantPrep.com

Please leave a review for this book!

Thank you for purchasing this resource.
If you would take a moment to kindly leave a
review on the website where you purchased this publication,
we would appreciate it.

Check out our collection of COGAT® prep books:

TABLE OF CONTENTS

INTRODUCTION

COGAT® GENERAL INFORMATION

- COGAT® stands for Cognitive Abilities Test®. It measures students' reasoning skills and problem-solving skills.
- It provides the teachers and administrators at your child's school with an assessment of your child's cognitive skills.
    - The test is sometimes used together with the ITBS™ (a.k.a. Iowa Test) to measure academic achievement.
- It is commonly used as a screener for gifted and talented programs.
    - Gifted and Talented (G&T) selection sometimes requires a teacher recommendation as well.
- The test is usually administered in a group setting.
- A teacher (or other school associate) administers the test, reading the directions. (Computerized versions of the test are also available.)
- Please check with your school / testing site regarding its testing procedures, as these may differ.

COGAT® LEVEL 9 FORMAT

- Students in third grade take the COGAT® Level 9.
- The test has 170 questions.
- The test is divided into 3 main parts, each called a "Battery." Each Battery has three question types. The chart below lists the number of questions by question type. (The two practice tests in this book have *approximately* this number of questions.) For example, the COGAT® has 22 Verbal Analogy questions.

VERBAL BATTERY	NON-VERBAL BATTERY	QUANTITATIVE BATTERY
Verbal Classification: 20 Questions	Figure Classification: 20 Questions	Number Puzzles: 16 Questions
Verbal Analogies: 22 Questions	Figure Analogies: 20 Questions	Number Series: 18 Questions
Sentence Completion: 20 Questions	Paper Folding: 16 Questions	Number Analogies: 18 Questions

- Often, schools administer one Battery per day, allowing approximately 45 minutes per Battery.
- Students have around 15 minutes to complete each question type (for example, students would have around 15 minutes to complete Verbal Analogies).
- See pages 6-11 for examples and explanations of each question type.

COGAT® SCORING

- Students receive points for correct answers. Points are not deducted for incorrect answers. (Therefore, students should at least guess versus leaving a question blank.)
- In general, schools have a "cut-off" COGAT® score, which they consider together with additional criteria, for gifted & talented acceptance. This varies by school.
- This score is usually at least 98%. (However, some schools accept scores 95% or even 85%.)
- A score of 98% means that your child scored as well as, or better than, 98% of children in his/her testing group.
- COGAT® scores are available for the entire test and can be broken down by Battery.
- Depending on the school/program, such a "cut-off" score may only be required on one or two of the Batteries (and not on the test overall).
- It is essential to check with your school/program for their acceptance procedures.
(The COGAT® Practice Tests in this book can not yield these percentiles because they have not been given to a large enough group of students to produce an accurate comparison / calculation.)

HOW TO USE THIS BOOK

1. Go over examples and explanations (p.6 - 11).

2. Do Practice Test 1.
- Do these questions together with your child, especially if this is your child's first exposure to COGAT®-prep questions.
  - Talk about what the question is asking your child to do.
- Questions progress in difficulty.
  - The first few questions are quite simple.
- Do at least one section (Verbal / Non-Verbal/ Quantitative) per day.
- Do not assign a time limit.
- Go over the answers using the Answer Key.
  - For questions missed, go over the answers again, discussing what makes the correct answer better than the other choices.

3. Do Practice Test 2.
- If your child progressed easily through Practice Test 1, then see how well your child can do on Practice Test 2 without your help.
- If your child needed assistance with much of Practice Test 1, then continue to assist your child with Practice Test 2.
- Do at least one section (Verbal / Non-Verbal/ Quantitative) per day.
- If you wish to assign a time limit, assign around 15 minutes per question type.
- Go over the answers using the Answer Key.
  - For questions missed, go over the answers again, discussing what makes the correct answer better than the other choices.

4. Go to our website, www.SavantPrep.com, for FREE 10 bonus practice questions (PDF format).

GET FREE 10 BONUS PRACTICE QUESTIONS (PDF) !
GO TO WWW.SAVANTPREP.COM AND GET THEM TODAY.

TEST-TAKING TIPS

- Ensure your child listens carefully to the directions, especially in the Sentence Completion section.
- Make sure (s)he does not rush through questions. (There is no prize for finishing first!) Tell your child to look carefully at the question. Then, tell your child to look at each answer choice before marking his/her answer.
  - If you notice your child continuing to rush through the questions, tell him/her to point to each part of the question. Then, point to each answer choice.
- If (s)he does not know the answer, then use the process of elimination. Cross out any answer choices which are clearly incorrect, then choose from those remaining.
- This tip/suggestion is entirely at your discretion. You may wish to offer some sort of special motivation to encourage your child to do his/her best. An extra incentive of, for example, an art set, a building block set, or a special outing can go a long way in motivating young learners!
- The night before testing, it is imperative that children have enough sleep, without any interruptions. (Think about the difference in your brain function with a good night's sleep vs. without. The same goes for your child's brain function.)
- The morning before the test, ensure your child eats a healthy breakfast with protein and complex carbs. Do not let them eat sugar, chocolate, etc.
- If you can choose the time your child will take the test (for example, if (s)he will take the test individually, instead of at school with a group), opt for a morning testing session, when your child will be most alert.

QUESTION EXAMPLES

- Here is an overview of the nine COGAT® question types.
- This section has <u>simple</u> examples, to introduce your child to test concepts.
  - Do these examples together with your child. Read him/her the directions.
- Below the questions are explanations for parents.

1. VERBAL ANALOGIES (VERBAL BATTERY)

- **Directions (read to child):** Here are two sets of words. Look at the first set of words. Try to see how they belong together. Then, look at the next set of words. The question mark shows where the answer is missing. Can you see which answer choice would make the second set of words go together in the same way that the first set of words goes together?

scales → fish : feathers → ?   A. pen   B. shark   C. beak   D. bird   E. fly

- **Explanation (for parents):** Your child must figure out how the first set is related and belongs together. Then, (s)he must figure out which answer choice would go with the first word of the second set so that the second set would have the same analogous relationship as the first set. (The small arrows demonstrate that the words go together.)

- One strategy is to try to define a "rule" to describe how the first set belongs together. Then, take this "rule" and use it with the second set. Look at the answer choices, and figure out which answer would make the second set follow your "rule."

- **Using the above question as an example, say to your child:**
In this question, we have "scales" and "fish." Scales are part of a fish. Also, more specifically, scales cover a fish. A rule would be, "the first thing covers the second thing." In the second set we have "feathers." Let's try the answer choices with our rule. A pen is not correct nor is a shark or a beak. "Bird" is correct because feathers cover a bird.

- Another similar strategy is to try to come up with a sentence to describe how the first set belongs together. Then, use this sentence with the second word. Look at the answer choices, and figure out which answer would make the sentence work with this second set. With both strategies, if more than one answer choice works, then you need a more specific rule/sentence.

- Make sure your child does not choose an answer simply because it *has to do with* the previous words or reminds them of previous words. In the above example, "beak" *has to do with* "feathers." "Shark" may *remind* them of the second word in the first set, "fish." These types of words are sometimes included in the answer choices, and students who do not look carefully at the question may choose them by mistake.

- The table below outlines the logic used in verbal analogies (on the COGAT®, as well as in verbal analogies, in general). We suggest reading the questions and answer choices to your child. This will help familiarize him/her with analogy logic.

Question (say below & each 'Choice' to child)	Choice 1	Choice 2	Choice 3	Choice 4	*Analogy Logic*
1. Fish -is to- Aquarium as Bird -is to- ?	Bowl	Butterfly	Cage ✓	Nest (note logic)	*Pet: Pet's Home (Made by People)*
2. Acorns -are to- Squirrel as Seeds -are to- ?	Grass	Bird ✓	Fish	Snake	*Animal: Animal's Food*
3. Calf -is to- Cow as Cub -is to- ?	Tiger ✓	Horse	Goose	Bull	*Baby: Adult*
4. Lion -is to- Fur as Snake -is to- ?	Lizard	Hair	Fangs	Scales ✓	*Animal: Animal's Covering*
5. Happy -is to- Sad as Wet -is to- ?	Damp	Clean	Water	Dry ✓	*Antonyms*
6. Tiger -is to- Cheetah as Butterfly -is to- ?	Bird	Bat	Moth ✓	Jaguar	*Similar Animals*
7. Small -is to- Little as Afraid -is to- ?	Dark	Tired	Haunted	Scared ✓	*Synonyms*

Question (say below & each 'Choice' to child)	Choice 1	Choice 2	Choice 3	Choice 4	Analogy Logic
8. Flower -is to- Bouquet as Kernel -is to- ?	Snack	Plant	Corn Cob ✓	Crop	Part: Whole
9. Ship -is to- Port as Car -is to- ?	Truck	Garage ✓	Marina	Wheel	Object: Location
10. Pencil -is to- Paper as Paint -is to- ?	Wall ✓	Color	Red	Light	Object: Object Used With
11. Lumber -is to- Fence as Paper -is to- ?	Log	Branch	Tree	Book ✓	Object: Product That Object Is Put Together To Make
12. Doctor -is to- Stethoscope as Carpenter -is to- ?	Boot	Builder	Cabinet	Hammer ✓	Worker Who Uses Object: Object
13. Cheese -is to- Refrigerator as Ice -is to- ?	Snow	Toaster	Freezer ✓	Cube	Object: Item Used to Store/Hold Object
14. Box -is to- Cube as Globe -is to- ?	Prism	Sphere ✓	Oval	Pentagon	Object: Similar Shape
15. Straw -is to- Juice as Spoon -is to- ?	Cereal ✓	Salad	Steak	Sandwich	Utensil: Object Utensil Is Used With
16. Egg -is to- Chicken as Milk -is to- ?	Chick	Cheese	Rooster	Cow ✓	Food/Drink: Source of Food/Drink
17. Large -is to- Enormous as Good -is to- ?	Bad	So-So	Happy	Super ✓	Degree

2. VERBAL CLASSIFICATION (VERBAL BATTERY)

• **Directions (read to child):** The three words in the top row are alike in some way. Look at the bottom row. There are five words. Which word in the bottom row goes best with the three words in the top row?

red   green   blue

A. paint   B. color   C. white   D. rainbow   E. shade

• **Explanation (for parents):** Together with your child, try to figure out a "rule" describing how the top words are alike and belong together. Then, apply the "rule" to each answer choice to determine which one follows it. If your child finds that more than one choice follows the rule, then a more specific rule is needed.

• **Using the above question as an example, say to your child:** In the top row, we have "red," "green," and "blue." What do these have in common? Each of these are colors. This is how they are alike. Which answer choice follows this rule of "colors?" The only answer choice that does is "white."

• Make sure your child does not choose a word simply because the choice *has to do with* the top three. For example, the other choices, especially Choice B ("color") have to do with the top three. However, "white" is the only choice that actually follows the rule.

Here is another example to demonstrate the importance of "rules" that are *specific*.

Atlantic   Indian   Arctic

A. American   B. Caribbean Sea   C. Gulf of Mexico   D. Pacific   E. ocean

In this example, the correct rule is "oceans of the world." (The world's oceans are the: Atlantic, Pacific, Arctic, Indian, and Southern.) However, a test-taker may at first come up with the rule "large body of water." If this happens, (s)he would have more than one answer choice that could be correct (Caribbean Sea, Gulf of Mexico, or Pacific). In this case, a more specific rule is needed. Here, (s)he should read the top three words again. In doing so, (s)he may realize that the top three words are large bodies of water that are *also* oceans. A more specific rule would be "ocean" or "oceans of the world." Therefore, the correct answer would be Choice D, "Pacific."

• Below are additional simple examples to introduce your child to classification logic. These will help familiarize him/her with basic classification logic. The classification logic/explanation is in the third column.

-Step 1: Read the three words on the left to your child. Tell him/her that these words belong together in some way.

-Step 2: Read the four words on the right to your child. Ask him/her which one of these goes best with the first three words. The answer has a check (✓). Following is a brief explanation of the question's logic in *italics*.

Question (read to child)	Answer Choices (read to child)	Classification Logic / Explanation
1. Cave / Hive / Web	Spider / Nest ✓ / Vet / Bat	*Animal Homes*
2. Butterfly / Ant / Bee	Worm / Horse / Bird / Dragonfly ✓	*Animal Types (Insects)*
3. Forest / Jungle / Desert	Tree / Valley / Rainforest ✓ / City	*Habitats*
4. Lemon / Grape / Apple	Strawberry ✓ / Farm / Sweet / Lettuce	*Kinds of Food (Fruit)*
5. Scientist / Nurse / Detective	Superhero / Teenager / Pilot ✓ / Fairy	*Jobs*
6. Sock / Skate / Boot	Slipper ✓ / Cap / Mitten / Toe	*Clothes/Shoes (Worn On Feet)*
7. Jet / Hot Air Balloon / Helicopter	Ship / Airport / Bird / Airplane ✓	*Transportation (Air Travel)*
8. Ruler / Scale / Measuring Tape	Thermometer ✓ / Number / TV / Pen	*Object Use (Used to Measure)*
9. Pillow / Blanket / Mattress	Towel / Chair / Sheet ✓ / Table	*Object Location (Found on Beds)*
10. Fire / Sun / Stove	Cookie / Toaster ✓ / Beach / Camp	*Object Characteristics (Give Heat)*
11. Planet / Ball / Globe	Country / Goal / Bubble ✓ / Racetrack	*Object Shape (Spherical)*

3. SENTENCE COMPLETION (VERBAL BATTERY)

• **Directions (read to child):** First, read the sentence. There is a missing word. Which answer choice goes best in the sentence? (Read the sentences and choices to your child. They may read along silently.)

As the water slowly evaporated, the bird bath became _____.
A. wet   B. empty   C. full   D. damp   E. clean

• **Explanation** Here, your child must use the information in the question and make inferences (i.e., make a best guess based on the information) and choose the *best* answer choice to fill in the blank.

• Note that Sentence Completion questions do not solely test vocabulary, but reasoning skills as well.

• Make sure your child pays close attention to every word in the sentence and to every answer choice. Have him/her re-read the complete sentence with the answer choice to ensure their choice makes the *most* sense compared to the other choices (the answer is B).

• Tell him/her to pay special attention to "negative" words like "not" or "no." Also, (s)he should watch out for words like "though," "although," "even though," which would show contrasting ideas.

4. FIGURE ANALOGIES (NON-VERBAL BATTERY)

• **Directions (read to child):** The pictures in the top boxes go together in some way. Look at the bottom boxes. One box is empty. Look at the row of pictures next to the boxes. These are the answer choices. Which one of these choices goes with the picture in the bottom box like the pictures in the top box go together?

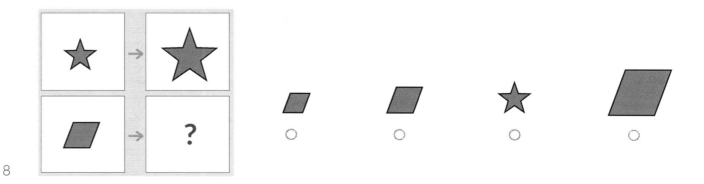

- **Explanation:** In the directions, the word "picture" means a "figure" consisting of one or more shapes/lines/etc. As with Verbal Analogies, try to define a "rule" to describe how the top set belongs together. With Figure Analogies, however, make your "rule" describe a "change" that occurs from the top left box to the top right box. Next, take this "rule" describing the change, and apply it to the bottom picture. Then, look at the answer choices to determine which one would make the bottom set also follow your "rule."

- **Using the question on the previous page, say to your child:** In the top left box, we see 1 star. In the top right box, we also see a star, but it has gotten bigger. Let's come up with a rule to describe how the picture has changed from left to right. From left to right, the shape gets bigger. On the bottom is a parallelogram. Let's look at the answer choices and see if any fit our rule. The first choice does not - the shape is smaller. The second choice does not - the shape is the same size. The third choice does not - it is a different shape. The last choice does - it is the same shape as the bottom box, but it is bigger.

- Below are examples of basic "changes" seen in Figure Analogies. Basic questions, like the example and #1-#9 below, have one "change." While more advanced questions have two changes (or changes that are not as obvious). The questions in the book's two practice tests will be much more challenging than these. See if your child can explain the changes below. At the end is a brief explanation.

1.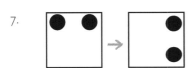

2.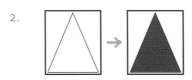

3.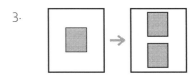

4.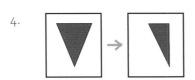

5.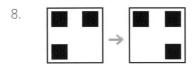

6.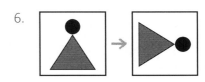

7.

8.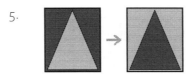

9.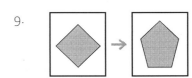

10.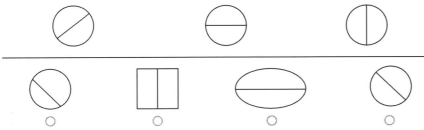

1. Size (gets smaller)
2. Color (white to gray)
3. Quantity (plus 1)
4. Whole to Half
5. Color Reversal
6. Rotation (clockwise, 90°)

7. Rotation (clockwise, 90°)
8. Rotation -or- Mirror Image / "Flip"
9. Number of Shape Sides (shape with +1 side)
10. Two Changes: Rotation (clockwise, 90°) and Color Reversal

5. FIGURE CLASSIFICATION (NON-VERBAL BATTERY)

- **Directions (read to child):** The top row shows three pictures that are alike in some way. Look at the bottom row. There are four pictures. Which picture in the bottom row goes best with the pictures in the top row?

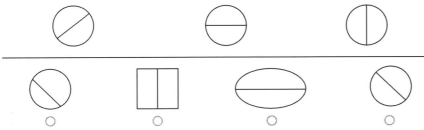

- **Explanation (for parents):** Together with your child, try to figure out a "rule" describing how the top pictures are alike and belong together. Then, apply the "rule" to each answer choice to determine which one follows it. If your child finds that more than one choice follows the rule, then a more specific rule is needed.

Here we see 3 circles. These circles are all divided in half. What is a rule that describes how they are alike? They are all circles that are divided in half. In the bottom row, which choice follows this rule? Choice 1 is a circle, but it's not divided in half. Choice 2 and 3 are divided in half, but they are not circles. Choice 4 is a circle divided in half. Choice 4 is the answer.

This list outlines some basic logic used in Figure Classification questions. (Practice test questions will be more challenging.)

How shapes are divided (Here, shapes are divided in quarters, with 1 part filled in.)	
How many sides the shapes have (Here, it is 4.)	
Do shapes have all rounded corners or straight corners? Or, no corners at all?	
Direction shapes are facing (Here, they face right.)	
Color / Design inside shape (Here, there are dots.)	
Shape quantity in each shape group (Here, 2 shapes in each group.)	
Shape group, with a set order to the group (Here, it's circle-diamond-square.)	
Direction of inside lines (Here, diagonal from upper left to lower right side.)	

6. PAPER FOLDING (NON-VERBAL BATTERY)

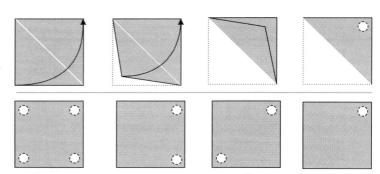

• **Directions (read to child):** The top row of pictures shows a sheet of paper. The paper was folded, then something was cut out. Which picture in the bottom row shows how the paper would look after its unfolded?

• **Explanation (read to child):** The first choice has too many holes. In the second choice, the holes are not in the correct position. The third choice has the correct number of holes and in the correct position. The last choice only shows the hole on top.

• **Tip:** It is common for children to initially struggle with Paper Folding - it is not an activity most children have much experience with. First, have a look at these Paper Folding examples. Then, demonstrate using real paper and scissors.

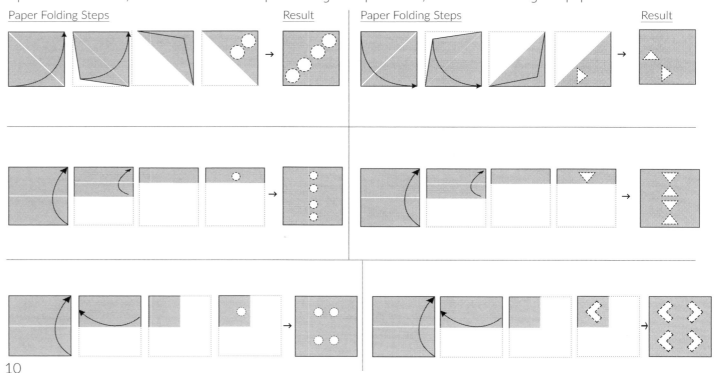

10

7. NUMBER SERIES (QUANTITATIVE BATTERY)

• Number Series questions can have 2 formats, an abacus or actual numbers.

• **Abacus Format Directions (read to child):** Which rod should go in place of the missing rod to finish the pattern?

• **Abacus Explanation (read to child):** Number Series questions come in two formats. Here, in the Abacus format question, we see that with each rod the number of beads decreases by 2. The rods go: 9–7–5–3–? This means that the missing rod needs 1 bead (Choice C).

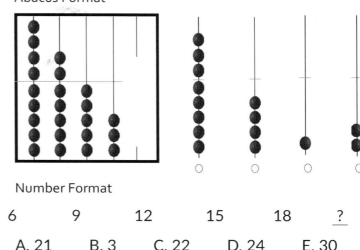

Abacus Format

Number Format

• **Number Format Directions (read to child):** The top row of numbers have made a pattern. Which answer choice would complete the pattern?

| 6 | 9 | 12 | 15 | 18 | ? |

A. 21   B. 3   C. 22   D. 24   E. 30

• **Number Format Explanation:** To help your child see the pattern, ask them to write the difference between each number and the next. Here, the difference between 6 and 9 is 3. The difference between 9 and 12 is 3. The difference between 12 and 15 is 3, and so on. In less challenging questions, this "difference" will be the same for each set of numbers. If the pattern is "add 3," then the answer is 21, because 18 +3 = 21. In more challenging questions, this pattern is not consistent with each set of numbers. See below:

30	29	27	24	20	15	?	Pattern: -1, -2, -3, -4, etc.; Answer: 9
7	2	1	7	2	1	?	Pattern: 7-2-1; Answer: 7
3	4	6	7	9	10	?	Pattern: +1, +2, +1, +2, etc; Answer: 12
5	0	6	0	7	0	?	Pattern: every other number +1; every other number = 0; Answer: 8

9. NUMBER PUZZLES (QUANTITATIVE BATTERY)

• **Directions:** Which number would be in place of the question mark so that both sides of the equal sign are the same?

• **Explanation:** These questions have two formats. The first example is a standard math problem. In the second example, your child needs to replace the black shape with the given number. Should your child have problems figuring out the answer of either format, (s)he can simply test each answer choice until they find the correct answer.

| 1. | 19 = ? + 5 | A. 5 | B. 24 | C. 20 | D. 4 | E. 14 |

| 2. | ? = ◆ - 8 | A. 0 | B. 1 | C. 2 | D. 3 | E. 4 |
| | ◆ = 11 | | | | | |

9. NUMBER ANALOGIES (QUANTITATIVE BATTERY)

• **Directions (same for both formats):** Look at the first two sets of numbers. Come up with a rule that both of these sets follow. Use this rule to figure out which answer choice goes in place of the question mark in the last set of numbers. (Number Analogies questions have two different formats.)

5	→	9
11	→	15
29	→	?

A. 25   B. 33   C. 4   D. 24   E. 32

• **Explanation (read to child):** Have your child figure out a rule that explains how the first number "changes" into the second number. It could use addition, subtraction, multiplication, or division. Have him/her write the rule by *each* pair. (S)he must make sure this rule works with *both* pairs. The rule for the first question is "+4," so 33 is the answer.

The rule for the second question (below) is "multiply by 3", so 30 is the answer.

[2 → 6]   [4 → 12]   [10 → ?]   A. 6   B. 3   C. 13   D. 30   E. 7

-PRACTICE TEST 1 BEGINS ON THE NEXT PAGE-

VERBAL CLASSIFICATION

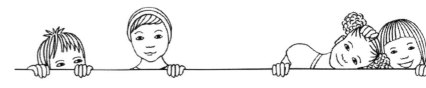

Directions (Read these aloud to your child. Your child may read along silently): The top row has three words that are alike in some way. In the bottom row are five words. Which word in the bottom row goes best with the words in the top row?

Explanation (for parents): A more detailed explanation and another Verbal Classification example question is on p.7. If you have not already, look over p.7 (later). Following is an excerpt. Together with your child, try to figure out a "rule" describing how the top words are alike and belong together. Then, apply the "rule" to each answer choice to determine which one follows it. If your child finds that more than one choice follows the rule, then a more specific rule is needed.

Example (read to child): In the top row are the words "Africa," "Europe," and "Asia." Let's come up with a "rule" to describe how these are each alike or how they belong together. These are all continents. Now, let's find the answer choice on the bottom that follows this same rule of "continents."

We have "India," "China," "Canada," "Middle East," and "North America." "North America" follows our rule because it is a continent.

1   **Africa**   **Europe**   **Asia**

        Ⓐ India   Ⓑ China   Ⓒ Canada   Ⓓ Middle East   Ⓔ North America

2   **broccoli**   **lettuce**   **carrot**

        Ⓐ strawberry   Ⓑ grape   Ⓒ celery   Ⓓ orange   Ⓔ cheese

3   **blue**   **brown**   **orange**

        Ⓐ dark   Ⓑ light   Ⓒ color   Ⓓ red   Ⓔ rainbow

4   **shoulder**   **hand**   **elbow**

        Ⓐ toe   Ⓑ wrist   Ⓒ neck   Ⓓ knee   Ⓔ spine

5 **ring**   **necklace**   **watch**

(A) gold   (B) bracelet   (C) silver   (D) glove   (E) hat

6 **March**   **May**   **August**

(A) month   (B) summer   (C) spring   (D) July   (E) Christmas

7 **lamp**   **torch**   **candle**

(A) wax   (B) flashlight   (C) yellow   (D) battery   (E) table

8 **mermaid**   **troll**   **unicorn**

(A) witch   (B) tiger   (C) costume   (D) dream   (E) glitter

9 **window**   **roof**   **door**

(A) wall   (B) branch   (C) street   (D) map   (E) neighborhood

10 **identical**   **alike**   **same**

(A) large   (B) unique   (C) matching   (D) single   (E) easy

11 **page**   **chapter**   **contents**

(A) librarian   (B) cover   (C) shelf   (D) internet   (E) alphabet

12 **bush**   **evergreen**   **palm tree**

(A) flower   (B) dirt   (C) garden   (D) growth   (E) lumber

13 **shorts**   **skirt**   **coat**

(A) suitcase   (B) drawer   (C) shoes   (D) fashion   (E) bag

14   **rise**   **expand**   **grow**

(A) slow   (B) increase   (C) reduce   (D) steady   (E) continue

15   **snow**   **teeth**   **polar bear**

(A) tongue   (B) acorn   (C) watermelon   (D) swan   (E) mint

16   **kayak**   **canoe**   **submarine**

(A) port   (B) marina   (C) truck   (D) jet   (E) ferry

17   **tea**   **soup**   **hot chocolate**

(A) popsicle   (B) yogurt   (C) ice cream   (D) coffee   (E) pancake

18   **pear**   **pineapple**   **peach**

(A) pebble   (B) apple   (C) pipe   (D) lettuce   (E) broccoli

19   **peak**   **top**   **crest**

(A) base   (B) wave   (C) tide   (D) floor   (E) ceiling

20   **strange**   **uncommon**   **odd**

(A) normal   (B) typical   (C) funny   (D) unusual   (E) late

VERBAL ANALOGIES

Directions (Read these aloud to your child. Your child may read along silently): The first set of words goes together in some way. In the second set of words, one word is missing. You must figure out which answer choice would go in place of the question mark so that the second set of words goes together in the same way that the first set of words goes together.

Explanation (for parents): A more detailed explanation and another example question is on p.6. If you have not already, look over p.6 (later). Following is an excerpt. Your child must figure out how the first set of words is related and belongs together. Then, (s)he must figure out which answer choice would replace the question mark so that the second set would have the same relationship as the first set.

Example (read this to child): "Wolf" and "howl." These are the words in the first set. (Together, try to come up with a "rule" describing how they are alike and go together.) The sound that a wolf makes is called a "howl." The first word is the animal. The next word is the name of the sound this animal makes. Let's look at the first word in the second set: "mouse." Remembering our rule, which choice goes best with "mouse?" What is the name of the sound that a mouse makes? "Squeak."

1   **wolf → howl : mouse →?**

    Ⓐ rat   Ⓑ roar   Ⓒ walk   Ⓓ nibble   Ⓔ squeak

2   **laces → shoe : zipper →?**

    Ⓐ scarf   Ⓑ jacket   Ⓒ sock   Ⓓ metal   Ⓔ foot

3   **Texas → state : Africa →?**

    Ⓐ capital   Ⓑ continent   Ⓒ city   Ⓓ Florida   Ⓔ geography

4   **scale → weight : thermometer →?**

    Ⓐ degrees   Ⓑ summer   Ⓒ temperature   Ⓓ clock   Ⓔ time

5   grape → vine : pear →?

Ⓐ green   Ⓑ leaves   Ⓒ apple   Ⓓ tree   Ⓔ fruit

6   hand → paw : fingernail →?

Ⓐ person   Ⓑ scratch   Ⓒ claw   Ⓓ hand   Ⓔ cut

7   boulder → rock : mountain →?

Ⓐ climb   Ⓑ ski   Ⓒ crystal   Ⓓ hill   Ⓔ cave

8   snake → lizard : parrot →?

Ⓐ chicken   Ⓑ panda   Ⓒ jungle   Ⓓ alligator   Ⓔ turtle

9   minute → time : inch →?

Ⓐ ruler   Ⓑ foot   Ⓒ mile   Ⓓ measure   Ⓔ length

10   ears → hear : tongue →?

Ⓐ food   Ⓑ lick   Ⓒ chew   Ⓓ taste   Ⓔ mouth

11   canoe → speedboat : wagon → ?

Ⓐ horse   Ⓑ truck   Ⓒ kayak   Ⓓ race car   Ⓔ farm

12   school → principal : ship →?

Ⓐ boat   Ⓑ sailor   Ⓒ captain   Ⓓ governor   Ⓔ crew

13   television → electricity : flashlight → ?

Ⓐ batteries   Ⓑ plug   Ⓒ light   Ⓓ candle   Ⓔ channel

14 here → hear : sale →?

    Ⓐ pale   Ⓑ sold   Ⓒ price   Ⓓ sail   Ⓔ sales

15 slice → loaf : petal →?

    Ⓐ stem   Ⓑ florist   Ⓒ nectar   Ⓓ flower   Ⓔ garden

16 monkey → jungle : sink →?

    Ⓐ bathroom   Ⓑ bedroom   Ⓒ towel   Ⓓ tub   Ⓔ animal

17 cool → frigid : large →?

    Ⓐ size   Ⓑ enormous   Ⓒ average   Ⓓ small   Ⓔ tiny

18 good → excellent : funny →?

    Ⓐ interesting   Ⓑ amusing   Ⓒ hilarious   Ⓓ laugh   Ⓔ nice

19 director → actors : conductor →?

    Ⓐ instruments   Ⓑ audience   Ⓒ stadium   Ⓓ theater   Ⓔ musicians

20 pigeon → flock : apple → ?

    Ⓐ fruit   Ⓑ orange   Ⓒ seed   Ⓓ bushel   Ⓔ bird

21 inhale → exhale : unite →?

    Ⓐ divide   Ⓑ connect   Ⓒ join   Ⓓ breathe   Ⓔ country

22 detective → investigation : scientist →?

    Ⓐ lab   Ⓑ experiment   Ⓒ chemical   Ⓓ teacher   Ⓔ measure

SENTENCE COMPLETION

Directions (Read these aloud to your child.):

In each question there is a missing word. First, read the sentence. Then, look below the sentence at each of the answer choices. Which choice would go best in the sentence?

Additional information (for parents): Page 8 provides Sentence Completion tips. If you haven't already, read p.8.

1   **The cheetah is a very _____ animal-it can run as fast a car driving on a highway.**

  Ⓐ easy   Ⓑ relaxed   Ⓒ swift   Ⓓ careful   Ⓔ clear

2   **This telescope allows us to see _____ objects in the solar system that we can't see with only our eyes.**

  Ⓐ close   Ⓑ direct   Ⓒ reachable   Ⓓ nearby   Ⓔ distant

3   **The rain was falling at a _____ of 5 inches every hour, which was enough to cause flooding.**

  Ⓐ rate   Ⓑ bucket   Ⓒ sprinkle   Ⓓ drop   Ⓔ splash

4   **If we _____ the cards instead of keeping them together, then it will take a long time to pick them up.**

  Ⓐ stack   Ⓑ scatter   Ⓒ pile   Ⓓ store   Ⓔ join

5   I will _____ the rabbit quietly because I do not want to scare it as I get closer.

    (A) leave   (B) drop   (C) approach   (D) see   (E) shove

6   Before making an important decision, it is necessary to _____ all the facts.

    (A) leave   (B) consider   (C) ignore   (D) forget   (E) create

7   As the number of _____ grew, the small town turned into a city.

    (A) teachers   (B) residents   (C) farms   (D) forests   (E) states

8   Sugar is an _____ ingredient in cookies, cakes, and other sweets.

    (A) overlooked   (B) incorrect   (C) essential   (D) optional   (E) unknown

9   I can _____ on my best friend Lee to help me if I ever need it.

    (A) rely   (B) pass   (C) follow   (D) improve   (E) dwell

10 We should keep a lookout and let the police know if we _____ anything strange.

(A) break   (B) observe   (C) arrest   (D) ignore   (E) fail

11 These last clues the detective examines should finally _____ who robbed the bank.

(A) conceal   (B) reveal   (C) hide   (D) direct   (E) save

12 Because she is _____ for her age, we trust her to babysit, even though she is only eleven.

(A) childish   (B) careless   (C) reckless   (D) foolish   (E) mature

13 You must _____ with the project if you want to finish it on time.

(A) stop   (B) disagree   (C) depart   (D) meet   (E) proceed

14 The doctor said it will take a month to _____ from my injury and play sports again.

(A) hurt   (B) weaken   (C) release   (D) recover   (E) break

15   It is surprising that despite being the youngest of my brothers, I am the
_____.

(A) tiniest   (B) tallest   (C) smallest   (D) youngest   (E) shortest

16   Because this city has earthquakes, the buildings are made to remain _____
during these natural disasters.

(A) damaged   (B) shaky   (C) stable   (D) rocky   (E) covered

17   In order to _____ rust, we keep a cover on our metal porch furniture after
we finish using it.

(A) prevent   (B) assist   (C) erase   (D) separate   (E) remove

18   The winters here are so_____ that people avoid going outside.

(A) mild   (B) moderate   (C) pleasant   (D) harsh   (E) merry

19   She loves to study_____ history to learn about events that occurred thou-
sands of years ago.

(A) late   (B) current   (C) modern   (D) recent   (E) ancient

20 After the sugar dissolves into the water, it is impossible to _____ the sweet flavor without adding more water.

(A) reduce   (B) increase   (C) taste   (D) raise   (E) gain

21 The elevator will go to the highest floor, then _____ to the basement.

(A) rise   (B) descend   (C) climb   (D) elevate   (E) lift

22 The magician snaps his finger to _____ you, while using his other hand to hide the coin without you noticing.

(A) avoid   (B) ignore   (C) hide   (D) distract   (E) delight

23 Her comment was so _____ , I have never heard anyone say something so odd.

(A) common   (B) peculiar   (C) normal   (D) loud   (E) quiet

24 This necklace is a _____ design that the jeweler created just for me.

(A) standard   (B) typical   (C) frequent   (D) boring   (E) custom

FIGURE CLASSIFICATION

Directions (read to child): The top row shows three pictures that are alike in some way. Look at the bottom row. There are five pictures. Which picture in the bottom row goes best with the pictures in the top row?

Explanation (for parents): A more detailed explanation of Figure Classification questions is on p.9. If you have not already, look over p.9 (later). Following is an excerpt. Together with your child, try to figure out a "rule" describing how the top pictures are alike and belong together. Then, apply the "rule" to each answer choice to determine which one follows it. If your child finds that more than one choice follows the rule, then a more specific rule is needed.

Example (read to child): Let's look at the pictures on the top row. We see 3 rectangles. Perhaps our rule could be "is a rectangle." However, this doesn't work because in the answer choices, there is more than 1 rectangle. Let's have a closer look at the top shapes. Inside the shape are solid black lines. Let's try the rule "has solid black lines inside." However, this doesn't work either because more than 1 choice has solid black lines inside.

Look at the *direction* of the solid lines in the top pictures. They are diagonal and go from the lower left corner to the upper right corner. Let's try that rule. We see that choice E has solid black lines going diagonally from the lower left corner to the upper right corner. (Note that choice A does not work because although it has diagonal lines, they are going the opposite direction. Choice D has diagonal lines going the correct direction, but the lines are dotted lines (not solid lines).)

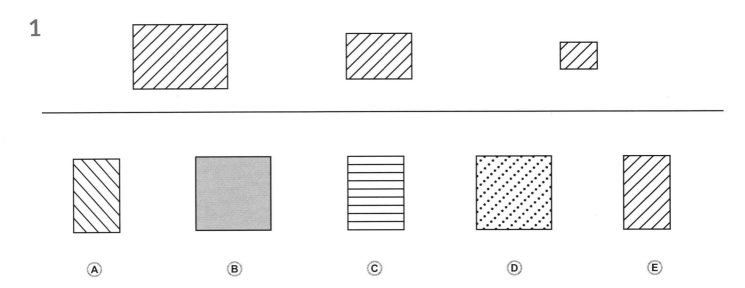

2

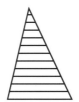  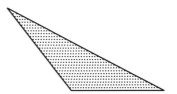

 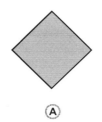 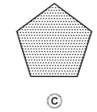  

   Ⓐ   Ⓑ   Ⓒ   Ⓓ   Ⓔ

3

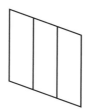 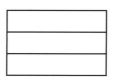

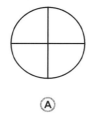 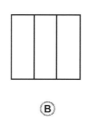 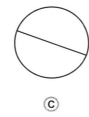 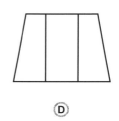 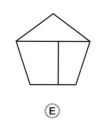

   Ⓐ   Ⓑ   Ⓒ   Ⓓ   Ⓔ

4

  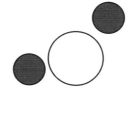 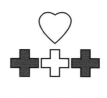 

   Ⓐ   Ⓑ   Ⓒ   Ⓓ   Ⓔ

5

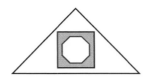 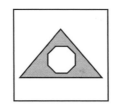 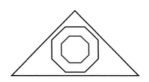

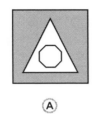  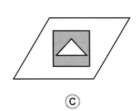 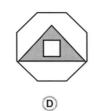 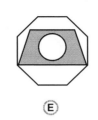

Ⓐ Ⓑ Ⓒ Ⓓ Ⓔ

6

  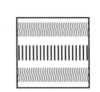

Ⓐ Ⓑ Ⓒ Ⓓ Ⓔ

7

 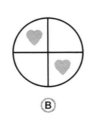  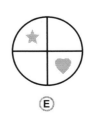 

Ⓐ Ⓑ Ⓒ Ⓓ Ⓔ

8

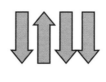 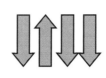 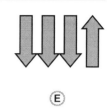

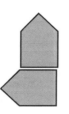 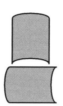 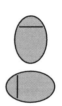

Ⓐ   Ⓑ   Ⓒ   Ⓓ   Ⓔ

9

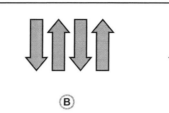 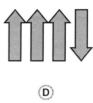

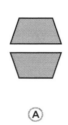   

Ⓐ   Ⓑ   Ⓒ   Ⓓ   Ⓔ

10

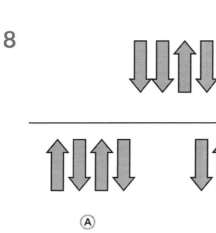

Ⓐ   Ⓑ   Ⓒ   Ⓓ   Ⓔ

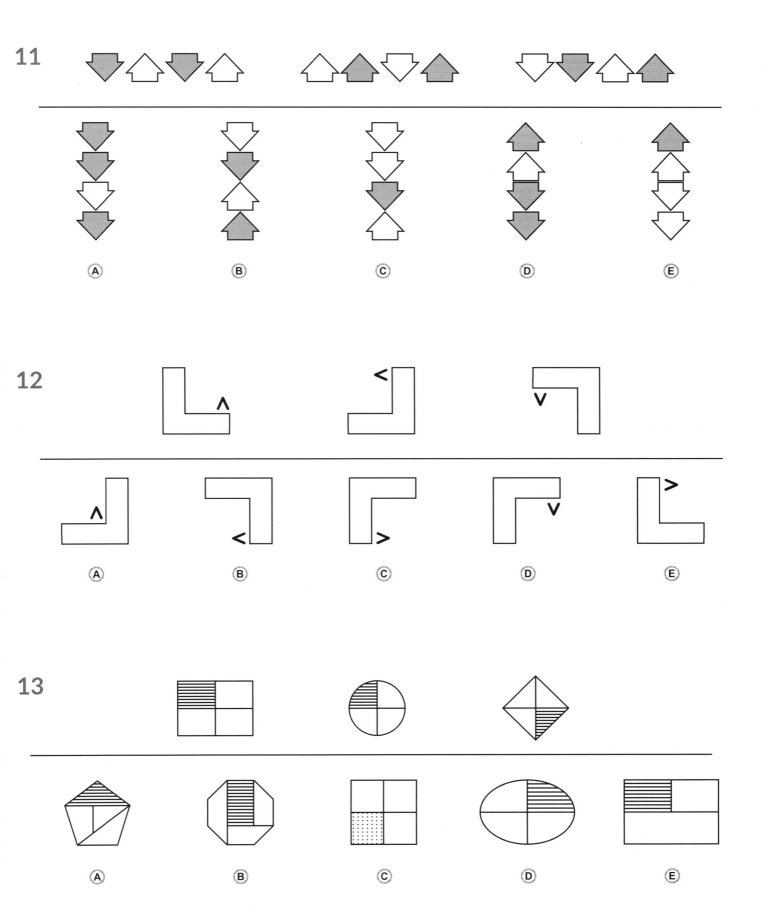

14

Ⓐ Ⓑ Ⓒ Ⓓ Ⓔ

15

Ⓐ Ⓑ Ⓒ Ⓓ Ⓔ

16

Ⓐ Ⓑ Ⓒ Ⓓ Ⓔ

17

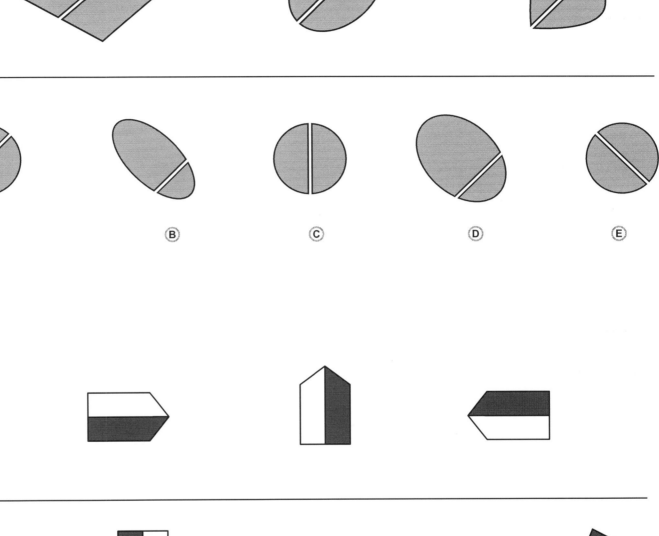

18

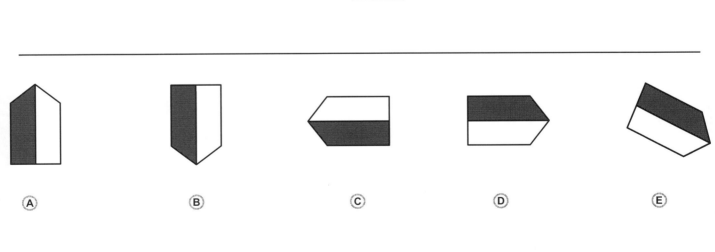

Directions (read to child): The pictures in the top boxes go together in some way. Look at the bottom boxes. One box is empty. Look at the row of pictures next to the boxes. These are the answer choices. Which one of these choices goes with the picture in the bottom box like the pictures in the top boxes go together?

Explanation (for parents): A more detailed explanation and a Figure Analogies example question is on p. 9. If you have not already, look over p.9 (later). Following is an excerpt. As with Figure Classification, try to define a "rule" to describe how the top set belongs together. With Figure Analogies, however, make your "rule" describe a "change" that occurs from the top left box to the top right box. Next, take this "rule" describing the change, and apply it to the bottom picture. Then, look at the answer choices to determine which one would make the bottom set also follow your "rule."

Example (read to child): Let's look at the picture top picture on the left side. We see a circle that is divided into black sections and white sections. Now, let's look at the top picture on the right side. How has the picture changed? Let's try to come up with a rule to explain the change. There is still a black and white circle. However, now, the colors have reversed. The white sections are now black, and the black sections are now white. Let's try the rule "the colors reverse."

On the bottom is a diamond with black sections and gray sections. Let's use our rule, "the colors reverse." Each answer choice has a diamond with black sections and gray sections. Look closely. Choice D is the same as the original diamond, but in Choice D all the black sections have become gray. All the gray sections have become black.

1

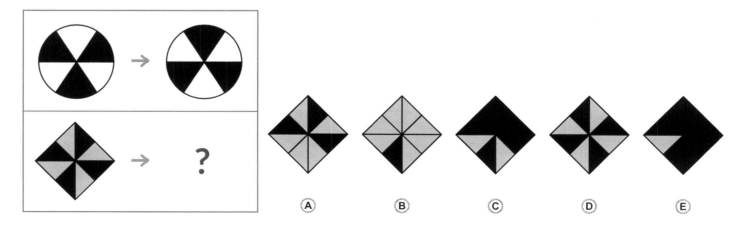

2

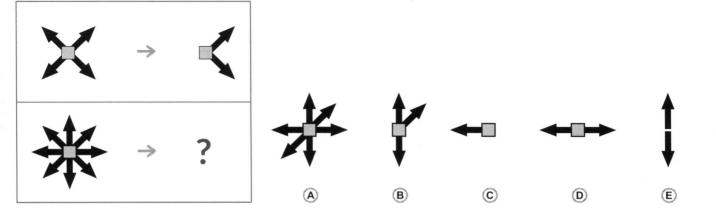

3

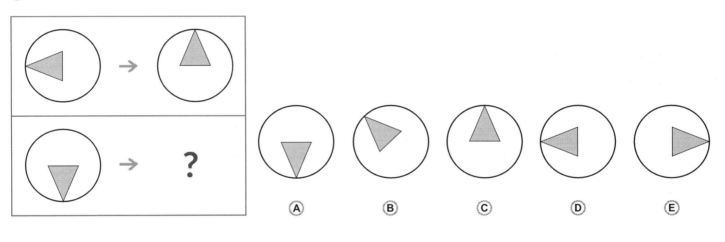

4

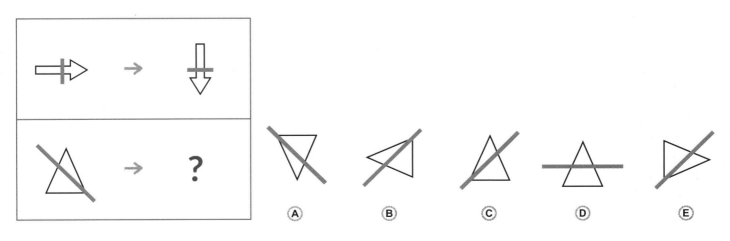

5

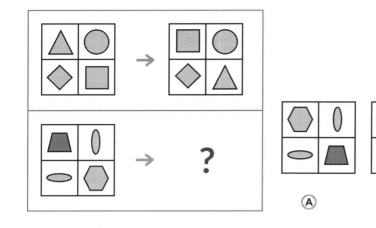

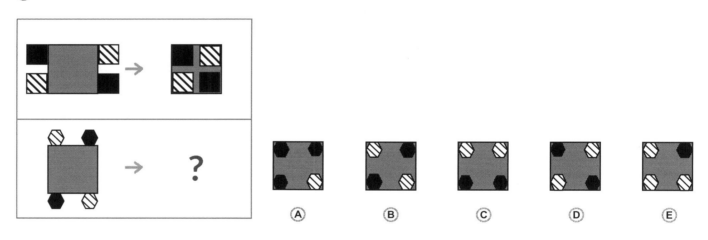

6

7

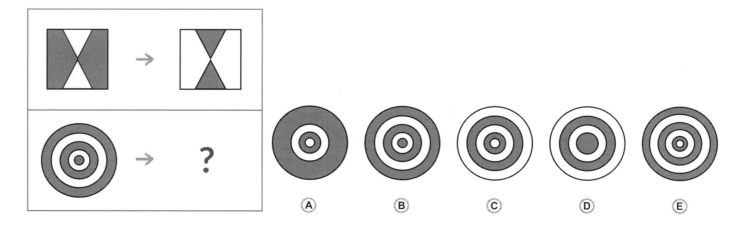

8

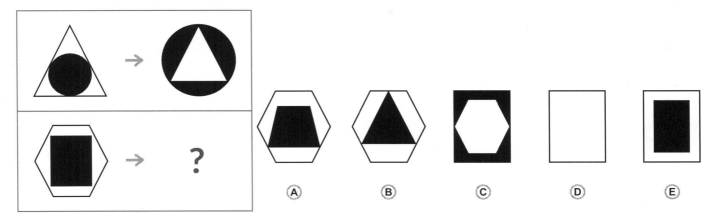

9

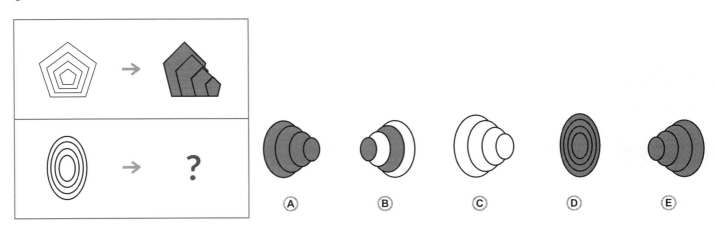

10

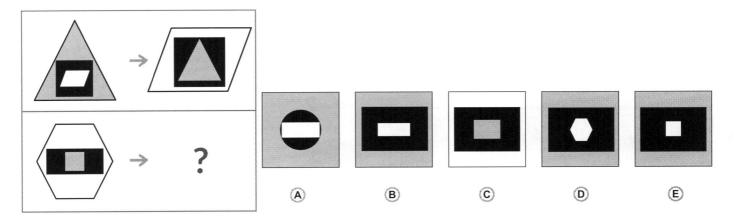

11

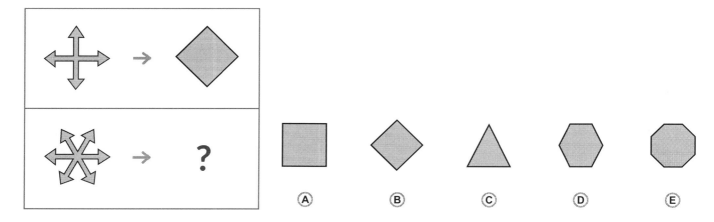

12

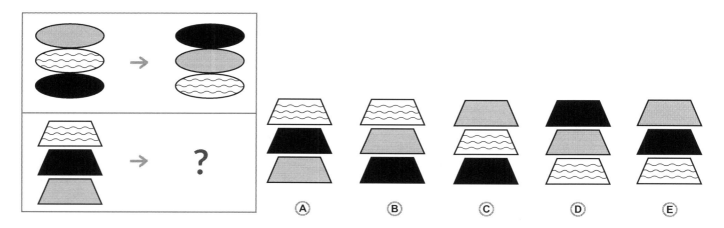

13

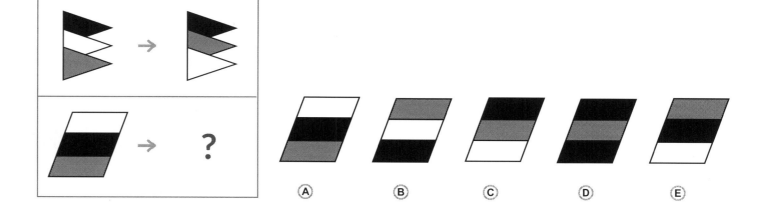

14

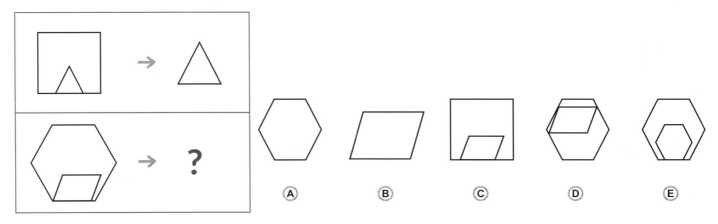

15

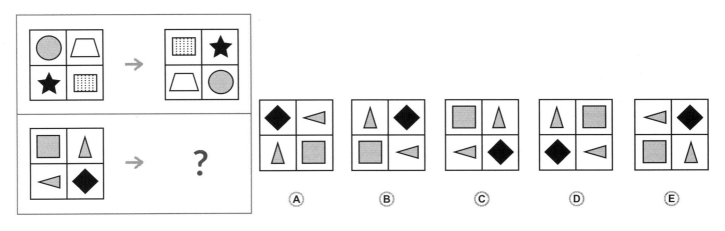

16

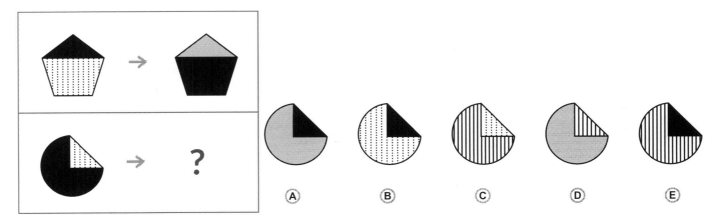

17

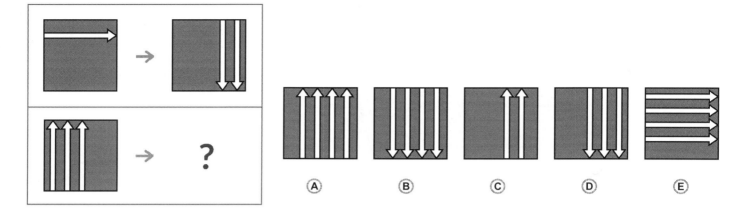

18

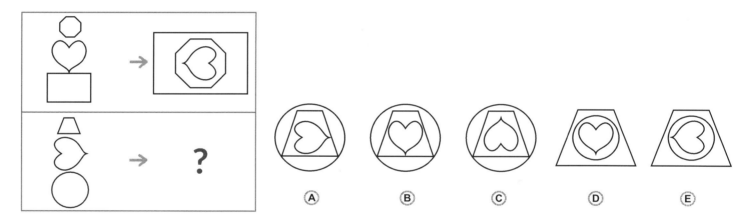

19

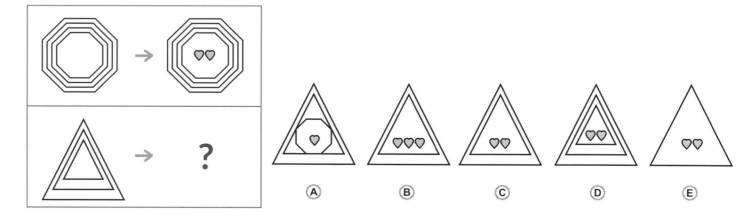

PAPER FOLDING

Directions (read to child): The top row of pictures shows a sheet of paper. The paper was folded, then something was cut out. Which picture in the bottom row shows how the paper would look after its unfolded?

Additional information (for parents): As explained earlier in the Introduction on p. 10, it is common for children to initially be "stumped" by Paper Folding. If your child needs help, then try demonstrating with real paper. Be sure to point out the number of holes (or other shapes) made and their position after opening the paper.

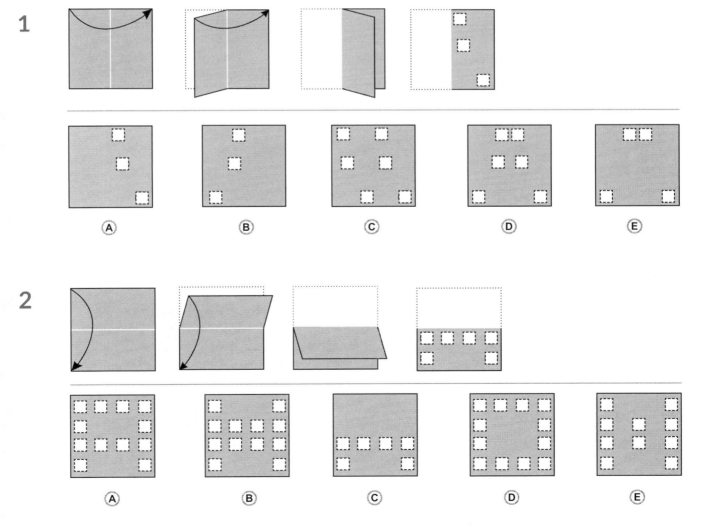

Parent note: Point out that #3 - #5 have been folded twice.

For #4, if your child chooses the wrong answer, point out that C is correct because the triangles "flip" in the correct direction.

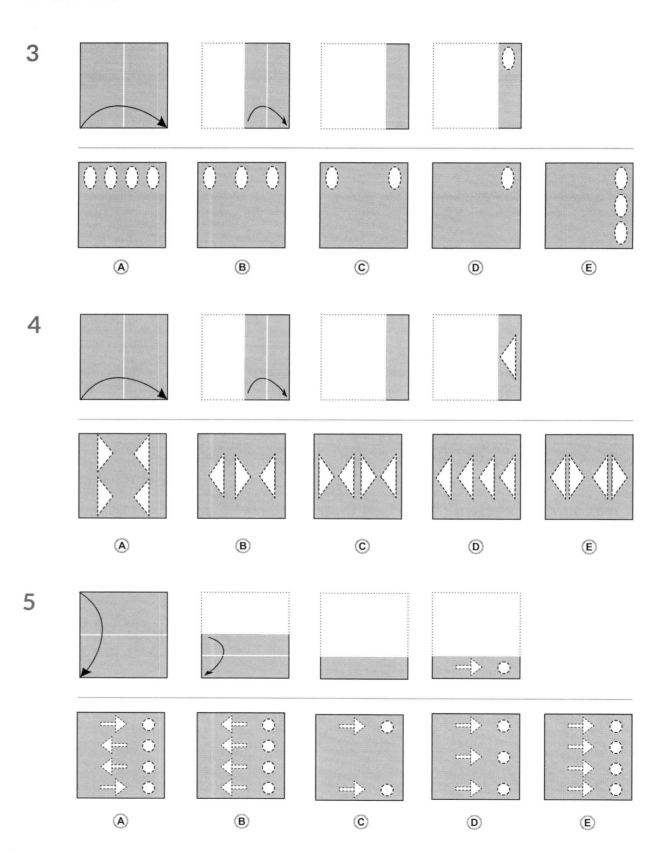

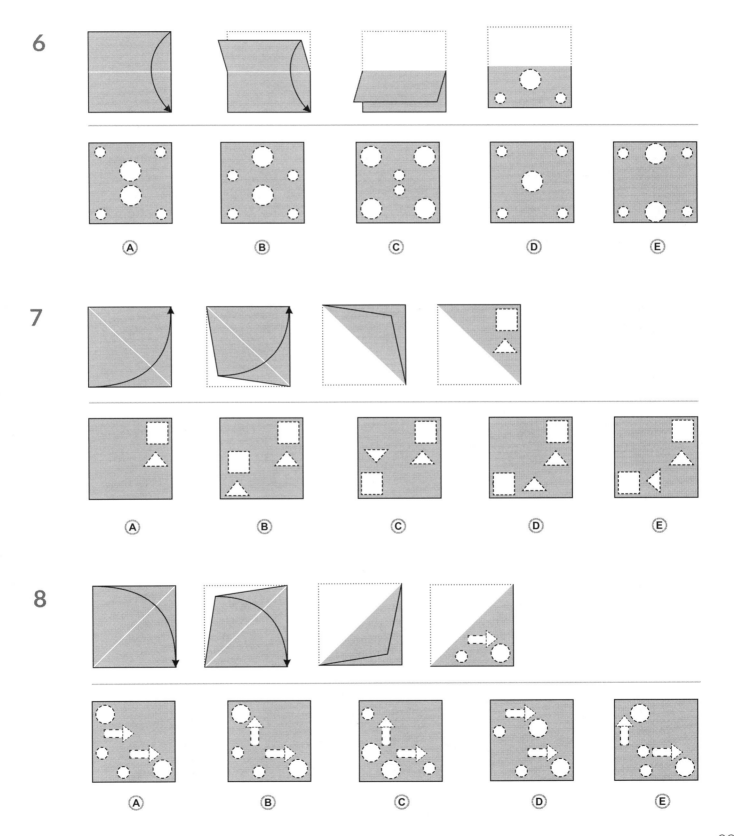

Parent note: In #9 - #11, point out that some shapes were made "along the fold."

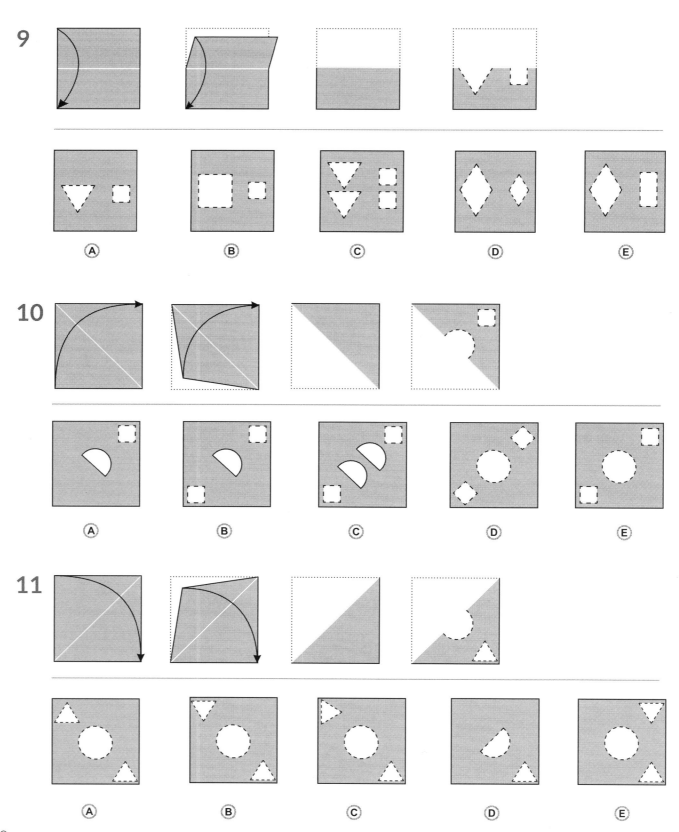

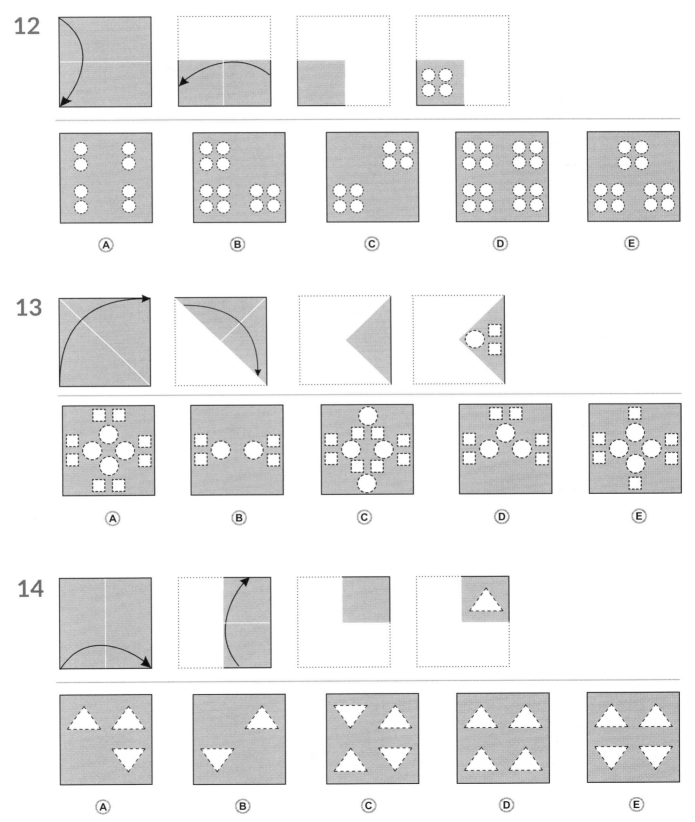

15

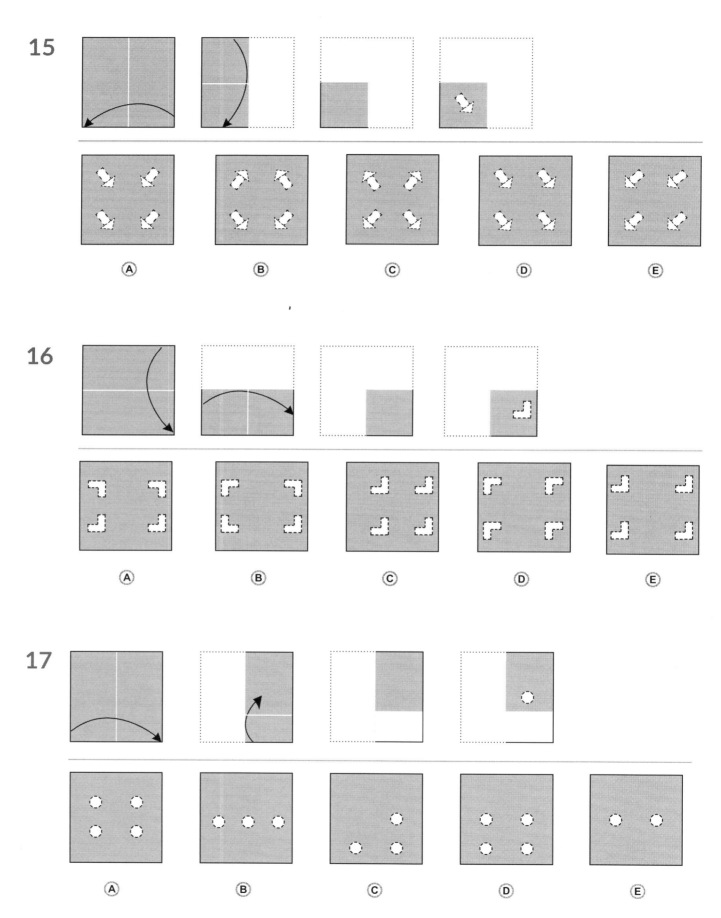

16

17

42

NUMBER PUZZLES

Directions (read to child): Look at the box that has the question mark. Which number would go here so that both of the sides of this equal sign (point to the equal sign) have the same amount?

Additional information (for parents): Be sure your child pays attention to the plus and minus signs. Some questions have two different signs. During the actual test, your child will most likely be able to use scratch paper. So, allow them to use scratch paper here if they wish. Page 11 has additional Number Puzzles tips.

Example: The left side of the equal sign has 45. Which answer choice do you need to put in place of the question mark so that the right side of the equal sign totals 45? 45 minus 26 equals 19. So, D is the correct answer.

1

| 45 | = | 26 | + | ? |

Ⓐ 71   Ⓑ 9   Ⓒ 18   Ⓓ 19   Ⓔ 29

2

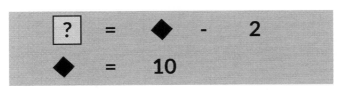

Ⓐ 12   Ⓑ 8   Ⓒ 6   Ⓓ 18   Ⓔ 20

3

$$13 \quad + \quad 19 \quad = \quad 52 \quad - \quad \boxed{?}$$

(A) 32   (B) 20   (C) 30   (D) 40   (E) 10

4

$$28 \quad = \quad 39 \quad - \quad 5 \quad - \quad \boxed{?}$$

(A) 28   (B) 34   (C) 11   (D) 16   (E) 6

5

$$15 \quad = \quad 31 \quad - \quad 29 \quad + \quad \boxed{?}$$

(A) 2   (B) 60   (C) 17   (D) 13   (E) 23

6

$$74 \quad = \quad 36 \quad + \quad 18 \quad + \quad \boxed{?}$$

(A) 20   (B) 10   (C) 56   (D) 54   (E) 18

7

$$48 \quad - \quad 9 \quad = \quad 62 \quad - \quad \boxed{?}$$

(A) 39   (B) 15   (C) 5   (D) 13   (E) 23

8

39 + 23 = 65 - [?]

(A) 16   (B) 13   (C) 62   (D) 3   (E) 49

9

80 = 54 - 8 + [?]

(A) 34   (B) 18   (C) 46   (D) 24   (E) 62

10

[?] = ◆ + 47

◆ = 15

(A) 52   (B) 62   (C) 32   (D) 15   (E) 22

11

[?] = ◆ x 7

◆ = 8

(A) 1   (B) 56   (C) 15   (D) 49   (E) 63

12

[?] = ◆ / 2

◆ = 18

(A) 16   (B) 36   (C) 9   (D) 8   (E) 20

13

$\boxed{?} = \blacklozenge \times 3$

$\blacklozenge = 7$

(A) 4   (B) 10   (C) 15   (D) 21   (E) 28

14

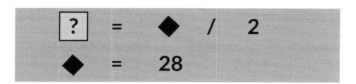

$\boxed{?} = \blacklozenge / 2$

$\blacklozenge = 28$

(A) 18   (B) 30   (C) 14   (D) 15   (E) 26

15

$\boxed{?} = \blacklozenge + 17 - 19$

$\blacklozenge = 38$

(A) 55   (B) 2   (C) 74   (D) 22   (E) 36

16

$\boxed{?} = \blacklozenge + 35 + 37$

$\blacklozenge = 7$

(A) 79   (B) 59   (C) 72   (D) 42   (E) 9

17

$\boxed{?} = \blacklozenge - 28 - 14$

$\blacklozenge = 42$

(A) 84   (B) 28   (C) 14   (D) 10   (E) 0

NUMBER SERIES

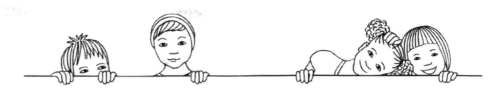

Directions (read to child): Here, you must try to figure out a pattern that the numbers have made. Which answer choice would complete the pattern?

Parent note: Some questions are in the form of #1 (an abacus). Some are in the form of #2 (a series of numbers). Page 11 has additional Number Series tips.

Example #1: Here is an abacus. The abacus rods have made a pattern. Below the rods is the number of beads that the rod has: 0 beads, 8 beads, 0 beads, 6 beads, etc. Here we see that every other rod has "0" beads. (The first, third, fifth, and seventh rods have 0.) Also, every other rod (the second, fourth, and sixth rod) have two less beads each time. If this is true, how many beads would the eighth rod have? What is four take away 2? It's 2. So, the rod with 2 beads is the answer.

Example #2: Do you see a pattern that the numbers in the series follow? With each number, you add 2. If this is true, then what would come after 40? It's Choice C, 42.

1

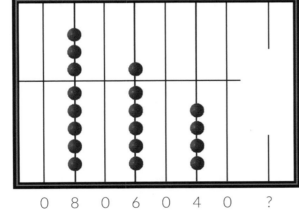

0 8 0 6 0 4 0 ?

1   2   3   7   5
Ⓐ   Ⓑ   Ⓒ   Ⓓ   Ⓔ

2   30   32   34   36   38   40   ?

○ 46   ○ 44   ○ 42   ○ 4   ○ 2

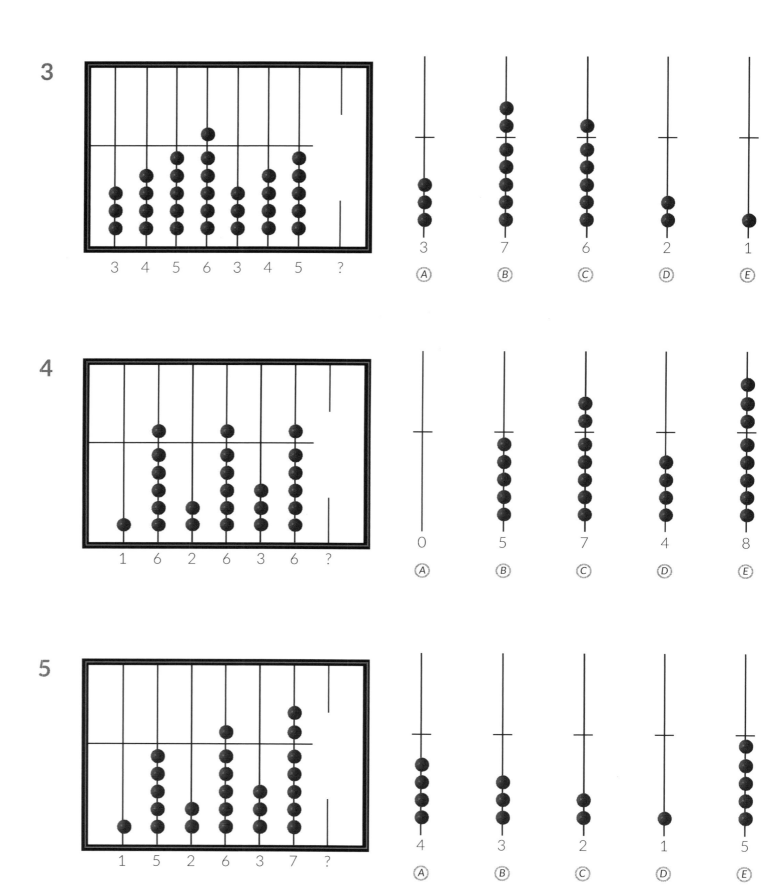

3

3 4 5 6 3 4 5 ?

(A) 3 (B) 7 (C) 6 (D) 2 (E) 1

4

1 6 2 6 3 6 ?

(A) 0 (B) 5 (C) 7 (D) 4 (E) 8

5

1 5 2 6 3 7 ?

(A) 4 (B) 3 (C) 2 (D) 1 (E) 5

6

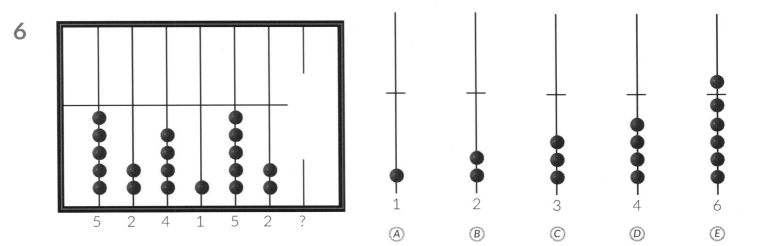

| 5 | 2 | 4 | 1 | 5 | 2 | ? |

| 1 | 2 | 3 | 4 | 6 |
| A | B | C | D | E |

7

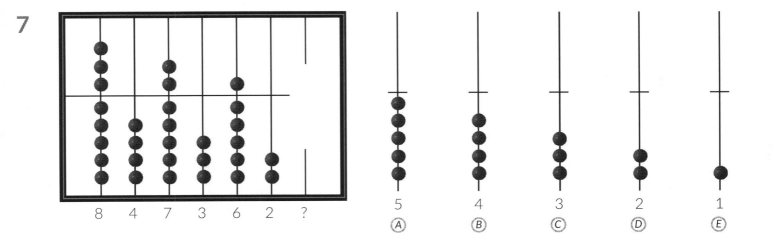

| 8 | 4 | 7 | 3 | 6 | 2 | ? |

| 5 | 4 | 3 | 2 | 1 |
| A | B | C | D | E |

8

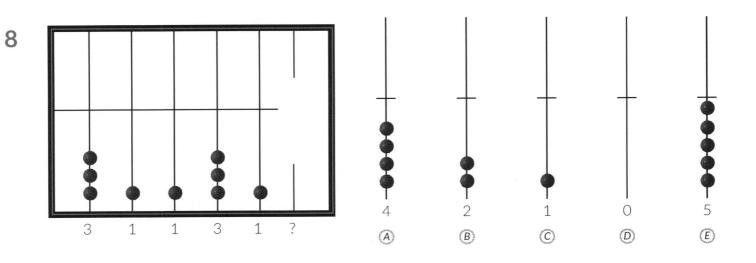

| 3 | 1 | 1 | 3 | 1 | ? |

| 4 | 2 | 1 | 0 | 5 |
| A | B | C | D | E |

9 23 26 29 32 35 38 ?

    (A) 43   (B) 42   (C) 41   (D) 45   (E) 37

10 5 6 8 9 11 12 ?

    (A) 10   (B) 17   (C) 15   (D) 14   (E) 13

11 31 30 28 27 25 24 ?

    (A) 22   (B) 12   (C) 23   (D) 20   (E) 21

12 5 7 10 12 15 17 ?

    (A) 19   (B) 18   (C) 24   (D) 20   (E) 22

13 10 12 9 11 8 10 ?

    (A) 13   (B) 2   (C) 3   (D) 8   (E) 7

14   **38**   **40**   **40**   **42**   **42**   **44**   **?**

(A) 40   (B) 58   (C) 46   (D) 42   (E) 44

15   **1.1**   **3.1**   **5.1**   **7.1**   **9.1**   **11.1**   **?**

(A) 14.1   (B) 12.1   (C) 13.1   (D) 1.1   (E) 10.1

16   **0.03**   **0.05**   **0.07**   **0.09**   **0.11**   **0.13**   **?**

(A) 0.15   (B) 0.14   (C) 1.15   (D) 1.17   (E) 0.16

17   **40**   **39**   **38**   **36**   **35**   **34**   **?**

(A) 33   (B) 32   (C) 36   (D) 30   (E) 29

18   **45**   **52**   **59**   **66**   **73**   **80**   **?**

(A) 84   (B) 86   (C) 87   (D) 94   (E) 88

19   **1.2**   **2.3**   **3.4**   **4.5**   **5.6**   **6.7**   **?**

(A) 7.7   (B) 6.8   (C) 8.9   (D) 7.8   (E) 7.1

NUMBER ANALOGIES

Directions (read to child): Look at the first two sets of numbers. Try to come up with a rule that both of these sets of numbers follow. Take this rule and try to figure out which answer choice goes in the place of the question mark to complete the third set of numbers.

Parent note: A more detailed explanation and a Number Analogies example question is on p. 11. If you have not already, look over p.11 (later).

Number Analogies questions are in two forms: the form of #1 (3 sets aligned vertically with boxes around the numbers) or in the form of #2 (3 sets aligned horizontally with no boxes).

Example #1: In the first set of numbers we see 2 and 3. In the second set, we see 4 and 5. How would you get from 2 to 3? How would you get from 4 to 5? In each, you add 1 to the first number. This could be the "rule" that both sets follow. Let's take this rule and apply it to the bottom set. What is the answer when you add 1 to 6? The answer is 7.

Example #2: In the first two sets, you have 3 and 6. In the next set you have 4 and 8. How would you go from 3 to 6? How would you get from 4 to 8? In both sets, you must multiply the first number by 2. (Or, you must double the first number.) This is the "rule." Take this rule and apply it to the last set. What is the answer when you multiply 5 by 2? The answer is 10.

1

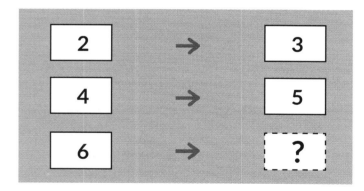

    Ⓐ 1   Ⓑ 9   Ⓒ 5   Ⓓ 7   Ⓔ 6

2   [3 → 6]   [4 → 8]   [5 → ?]

    Ⓐ 2   Ⓑ 5   Ⓒ 10   Ⓓ 25   Ⓔ 12

3

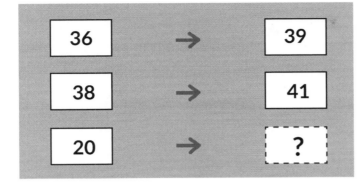

36	→	39
38	→	41
20	→	?

Ⓐ 23   Ⓑ 17   Ⓒ 3   Ⓓ 60   Ⓔ 44

4

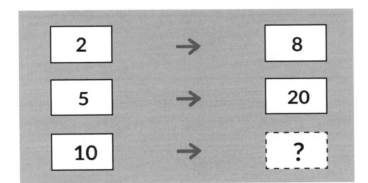

2	→	8
5	→	20
10	→	?

Ⓐ 16   Ⓑ 24   Ⓒ 4   Ⓓ 14   Ⓔ 40

5

42	→	37
16	→	11
39	→	?

Ⓐ 44   Ⓑ 34   Ⓒ 5   Ⓓ 16   Ⓔ 35

6

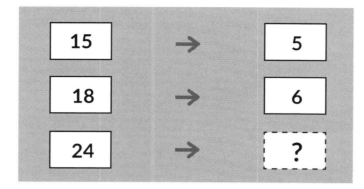

Ⓐ 3   Ⓑ 21   Ⓒ 27   Ⓓ 8   Ⓔ 7

7

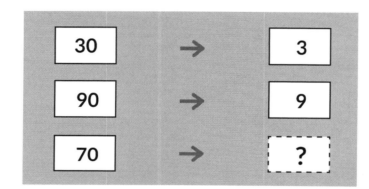

Ⓐ 7   Ⓑ 10   Ⓒ 77   Ⓓ 63   Ⓔ 12

8

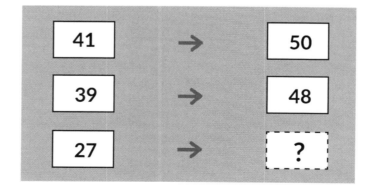

Ⓐ 3   Ⓑ 9   Ⓒ 36   Ⓓ 39   Ⓔ 18

9   [10 → 5]   [18 → 9]   [14 → ?]

Ⓐ 2   Ⓑ 12   Ⓒ 16   Ⓓ 14   Ⓔ 7

10   [37 → 29]   [47 → 39]   [52 → ?]

Ⓐ 60   Ⓑ 40   Ⓒ 59   Ⓓ 44   Ⓔ 50

11   [35 → 29]   [24 → 18]   [52 → ?]

Ⓐ 24   Ⓑ 46   Ⓒ 32   Ⓓ 8   Ⓔ 60

12   [27 → 34]   [39 → 46]   [28 → ?]

Ⓐ 21   Ⓑ 35   Ⓒ 7   Ⓓ 4   Ⓔ 14

13   [42 → 34]   [11 → 3]   [24 → ?]

Ⓐ 16   Ⓑ 8   Ⓒ 32   Ⓓ 3   Ⓔ 50

14 [2 → 12]   [4 → 24]   [5 → ?]

Ⓐ 11   Ⓑ 1   Ⓒ 6   Ⓓ 12   Ⓔ 30

15 [18 → 9]   [31 → 22]   [11 → ?]

Ⓐ 12   Ⓑ 99   Ⓒ 2   Ⓓ 40   Ⓔ 8

16 [36 → 9]   [24 → 6]   [32 → ?]

Ⓐ 24   Ⓑ 28   Ⓒ 36   Ⓓ 8   Ⓔ 16

17 [25 → 18]   [38 → 31]   [56 → ?]

Ⓐ 57   Ⓑ 62   Ⓒ 49   Ⓓ 8   Ⓔ 7

18 [24 → 8]   [33 → 11]   [12 → ?]

Ⓐ 3   Ⓑ 4   Ⓒ 2   Ⓓ 36   Ⓔ 9

- PRACTICE TEST 2 BEGINS ON THE NEXT PAGE -

VERBAL CLASSIFICATION   Directions: The top row has three words that are alike in some way. On the bottom row are five words. Which word on the bottom row goes best with the words on the top row?

1   **goldfish**   **shark**   **eel**

   (A) whale   (B) coral   (C) crab   (D) catfish   (E) otter

2   **soccer**   **baseball**   **basketball**

   (A) bat   (B) volleyball   (C) team   (D) coach   (E) tournament

3   **pencil**   **notebook**   **ruler**

   (A) eraser   (B) remote   (C) TV   (D) bus   (E) alarm clock

4   **microwave**   **oven**   **grill**

   (A) freezer   (B) refrigerator   (C) stove   (D) pan   (E) meal

5   **flute**   **guitar**   **piano**

   (A) music   (B) instrument   (C) harp   (D) microphone   (E) musician

6   **trumpet**   **flute**   **horn**

   (A) violin   (B) drums   (C) radio   (D) tuba   (E) concert

7   **Italy**   **Mexico**   **China**

   (A) Russia   (B) Asia   (C) Atlantic   (D) New York   (E) South America

8   **strong**   **sturdy**   **mighty**

   (A) straight   (B) powerful   (C) weak   (D) full   (E) wide

9   **taste**   **sight**   **touch**

   (A) smell   (B) eat   (C) dance   (D) hands   (E) nose

10   **pyramid**   **cube**   **cone**

   (A) rectangle   (B) sphere   (C) square   (D) line   (E) shape

11   **Mexican**   **Canadian**   **Japanese**

Ⓐ New York   Ⓑ Tokyo   Ⓒ German   Ⓓ Asian   Ⓔ Brazil

12   **hill**   **valley**   **mountain**

Ⓐ city   Ⓑ tree   Ⓒ canyon   Ⓓ state   Ⓔ monument

13   **cow**   **monkey**   **dolphin**

Ⓐ crow   Ⓑ gecko   Ⓒ beaver   Ⓓ catfish   Ⓔ ant

14   **scarf**   **mittens**   **boots**

Ⓐ jacket   Ⓑ swimsuit   Ⓒ umbrella   Ⓓ purse   Ⓔ hanger

15   **wagon**   **bike**   **truck**

Ⓐ airplane   Ⓑ train   Ⓒ helicopter   Ⓓ glider   Ⓔ tugboat

16   **trail**   **track**   **sidewalk**

Ⓐ highway   Ⓑ race   Ⓒ exercise   Ⓓ path   Ⓔ shoes

17   **crow**   **tire**   **night**

Ⓐ sun   Ⓑ coal   Ⓒ milk   Ⓓ apple   Ⓔ ruby

18   **swamp**   **harbor**   **creek**

Ⓐ water   Ⓑ swimming pool   Ⓒ shower   Ⓓ float   Ⓔ lake

19   **pair**   **partner**   **couple**

Ⓐ triplet   Ⓑ twin   Ⓒ single   Ⓓ one   Ⓔ bunch

20   **end**   **last**   **conclusion**

Ⓐ section   Ⓑ part   Ⓒ answer   Ⓓ copy   Ⓔ final

VERBAL ANALOGIES   Directions: The first set of words goes together in some way. Which answer choice would go in place of the question mark so that the second set of words goes together in the same way as the first set?

1   **empty → full : near →?**

Ⓐ long   Ⓑ far   Ⓒ close   Ⓓ miles   Ⓔ travel

2   **brush → painter : hammer →?**

Ⓐ nail   Ⓑ teacher   Ⓒ tool   Ⓓ carpenter   Ⓔ paint

3   **bouquet → flower : book →?**

Ⓐ library   Ⓑ read   Ⓒ dictionary   Ⓓ page   Ⓔ florist

4   **month → year : player →?**

Ⓐ score   Ⓑ coach   Ⓒ calendar   Ⓓ tennis   Ⓔ team

5   **bee → honey: chicken →?**

Ⓐ rooster   Ⓑ farm   Ⓒ egg   Ⓓ hen   Ⓔ omelet

6   **shovel → digs : towel →?**

Ⓐ tubs   Ⓑ legs   Ⓒ dries   Ⓓ paper   Ⓔ waters

7   **float → swim : stand →?**

Ⓐ still   Ⓑ walk   Ⓒ sit   Ⓓ seat   Ⓔ lap

8   **warm → burning : quiet →?**

Ⓐ calm   Ⓑ cool   Ⓒ silent   Ⓓ peaceful   Ⓔ hot

9   **baseball → bat : nail →?**

Ⓐ racket   Ⓑ hammer   Ⓒ scissors   Ⓓ saw   Ⓔ carpenter

10   **necklace → jewelry: sofa →?**

Ⓐ chair   Ⓑ ring   Ⓒ pillow   Ⓓ furniture   Ⓔ sit

11   **pencil → sketch : brush →?**

    Ⓐ paint   Ⓑ crayon   Ⓒ artist   Ⓓ paper   Ⓔ marker

12   **carpenter → build : mechanic →?**

    Ⓐ wrench   Ⓑ repair   Ⓒ garage   Ⓓ walk   Ⓔ race

13   **kick → ball : climb →?**

    Ⓐ goal   Ⓑ steep   Ⓒ gym   Ⓓ weight   Ⓔ ladder

14   **state → country : tree →?**

    Ⓐ root   Ⓑ forest   Ⓒ pine   Ⓓ timber   Ⓔ branch

15   **below → under : lucky →?**

    Ⓐ happy   Ⓑ chance   Ⓒ fortunate   Ⓓ above   Ⓔ free

16   **car → vehicle : bee →?**

    Ⓐ grasshopper   Ⓑ sting   Ⓒ hive   Ⓓ animal   Ⓔ honey

17   **scarf → jacket : sheet →?**

    Ⓐ pillow   Ⓑ laundry   Ⓒ raincoat   Ⓓ room   Ⓔ warmth

18   **tomorrow → yesterday : future →?**

    Ⓐ day   Ⓑ present   Ⓒ date   Ⓓ first   Ⓔ past

19   **virus → sickness : rain →?**

    Ⓐ wet   Ⓑ umbrella   Ⓒ flood   Ⓓ cold   Ⓔ water

Directions: First, read the sentence. A word is missing. Then, look below the sentence at each of the answer choices. Which choice would go best in the sentence?

1   **We have to _____ the number of tickets because the theater only has a small number of seats.**

Ⓐ enlarge   Ⓑ limit   Ⓒ allow   Ⓓ assist   Ⓔ increase

2   **After realizing that we were at the wrong house, my dad had to _____ the car to exit the driveway.**

Ⓐ brake   Ⓑ race   Ⓒ mend   Ⓓ advance   Ⓔ reverse

3   **If more people sign up for the camping trip, then we will need to bring _____ tents.**

Ⓐ fewer   Ⓑ miniature   Ⓒ invisible   Ⓓ reduced   Ⓔ additional

4   **Since my bike is so old and rusty, I _____ the shiny, new bike my friend has.**

Ⓐ request   Ⓑ refuse   Ⓒ respect   Ⓓ envy   Ⓔ judge

5   **The bakery opened its doors, hoping the smell of fresh donuts would _____ customers.**

Ⓐ attract   Ⓑ release   Ⓒ carry   Ⓓ sniff   Ⓔ expand

6 My brother couldn't _____ if he had turned off the stove before leaving, so he had to go back and check.

(A) display   (B) recall   (C) forget   (D) calculate   (E) recite

7 Because that factory already _____ cars, it will be easy for them to make trucks.

(A) separates   (B) destroys   (C) races   (D) manufactures   (E) charges

8 The _____ reason he plays tennis so well is that he practices each day.

(A) primary   (B) popular   (C) previous   (D) lively   (E) cheerful

9 The basketball player's height clearly gave her an _____ over the other players who were shorter.

(A) injury   (B) obstacle   (C) option   (D) advantage   (E) overtime

10 I did not _____ to sleep so late, but I forgot to set my alarm clock.

(A) forget   (B) intend   (C) remember   (D) dislike   (E) nap

11 A blinking yellow traffic light_____ that drivers may continue carefully through the intersection.

(A) hides   (B) indicates   (C) realizes   (D) conceals   (E) strengthens

12 Shorts and flip-flops are not _____ clothes to wear to a fancy restaurant.

(A) suitable   (B) awkward   (C) simple   (D) clean   (E) plain

13 At the end of the school year, the students are quite _____ to start their summer vacations.

(A) eager   (B) reluctant   (C) unlikely   (D) doubtful   (E) hesitant

14 After completing the driver safety course, you will get a _____ which will allow you to drive with an adult.

(A) test   (B) permit   (C) trial   (D) vehicle   (E) warning

15 Instead of happening all at once, there is a _____ change in the temperature as the seasons change from fall to winter.

(A) sudden   (B) bright   (C) rapid   (D) short   (E) gradual

16　The book told the _____ story of the town during the war.

(A) mild　　　(B) fortunate　(C) tragic　　(D) cheery　　(E) delightful

17　The salesman will try to _____ my parents to purchase the most expensive car.

(A) prevent　(B) discourage　(C) persuade　(D) restrict　(E) limit

18　When our soccer team won the championship, it was such a surprise because the other team had won the five _____ years.

(A) future　　(B) previous　(C) next　　(D) upcoming　(E) following

19　The hotel does not have any _____ rooms, so we'll need to stay somewhere else.

(A) available　(B) full　(C) occupied　(D) useless　(E) crowded

20　The field stretches for miles and is so _____ that you cannot see the end.

(A) compact　(B) vast　(C) sheltered　(D) fenced　(E) flat

FIGURE CLASSIFICATION

Directions: The top row shows three pictures that are alike in some way. On the bottom row are five pictures. Which picture on the bottom row goes best with the pictures in the top row?

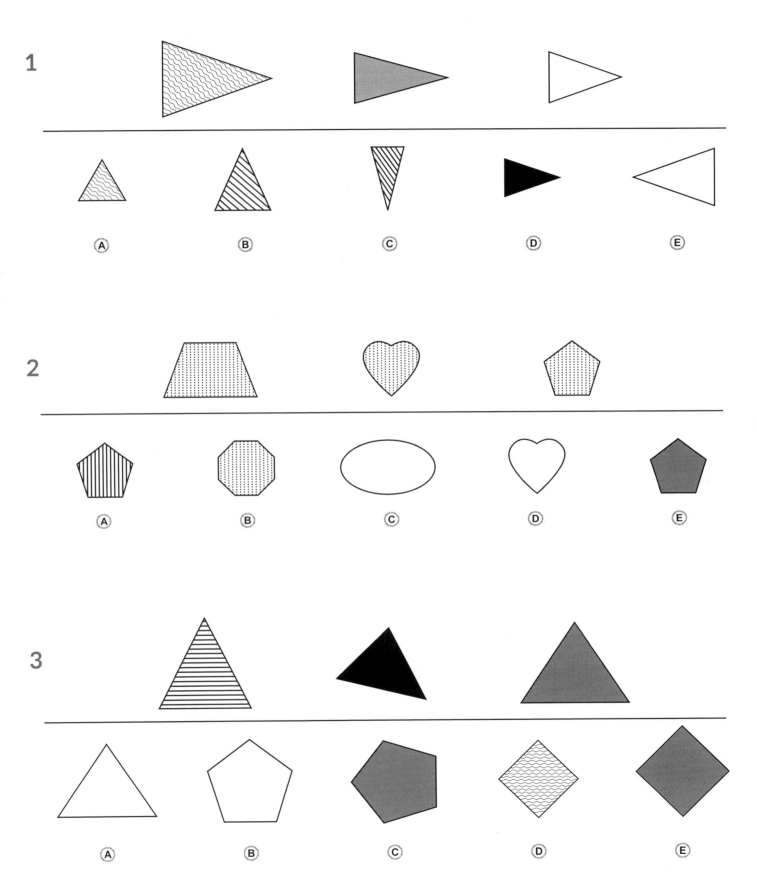

1

A   B   C   D   E

2

A   B   C   D   E

3

A   B   C   D   E

4

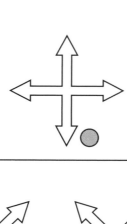 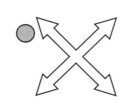 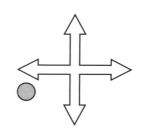

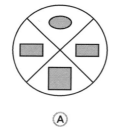 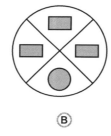 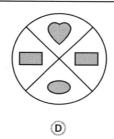  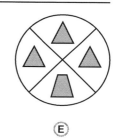

(A)   (B)   (C)   (D)   (E)

5

  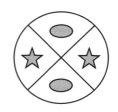

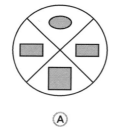 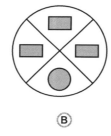 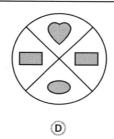  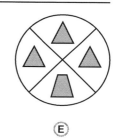

(A)   (B)   (C)   (D)   (E)

6

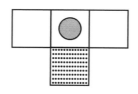 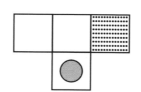 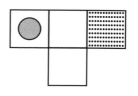

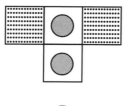 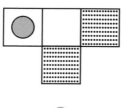 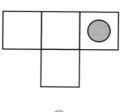 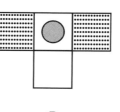 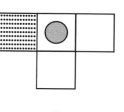

(A)   (B)   (C)   (D)   (E)

7

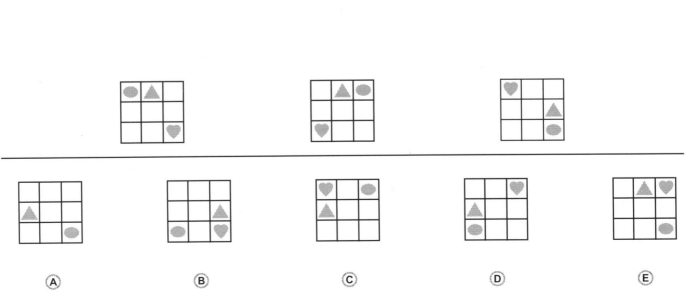

8

9

10

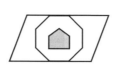  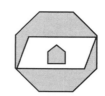

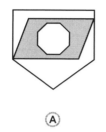  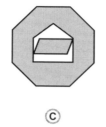 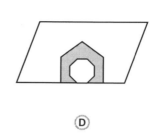 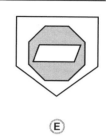

(A) (B) (C) (D) (E)

11

   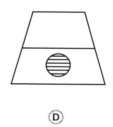 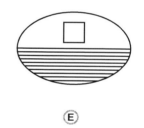

(A) (B) (C) (D) (E)

12

  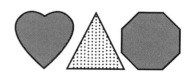

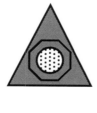   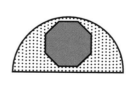

(A) (B) (C) (D) (E)

68

13

 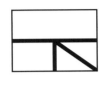  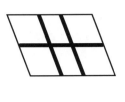

Ⓐ Ⓑ Ⓒ Ⓓ Ⓔ

14

Ⓐ Ⓑ Ⓒ Ⓓ Ⓔ

15

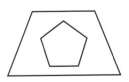

    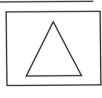

Ⓐ Ⓑ Ⓒ Ⓓ Ⓔ

16

17

18

70

FIGURE ANALOGIES

Directions: The top set of pictures goes together in some way. The bottom set is missing a picture. Which answer choice would make the bottom set go together in the same way the top set does?

1

2

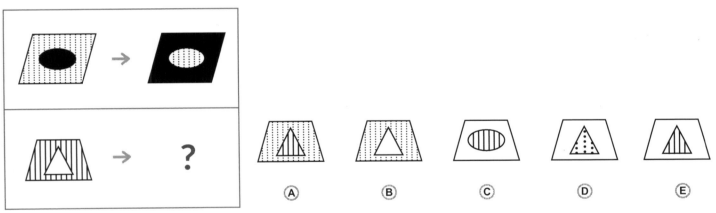

3

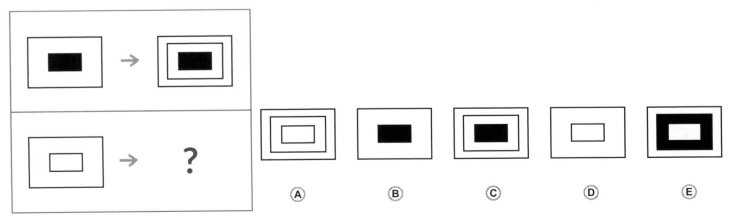

4

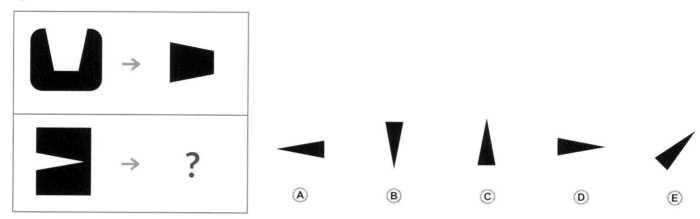

5

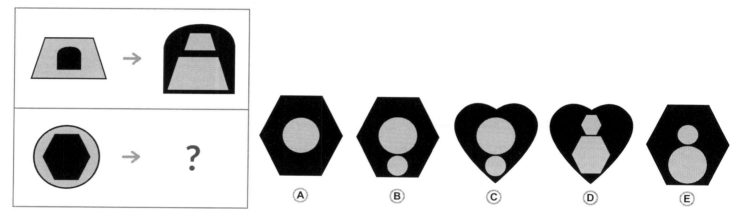

6

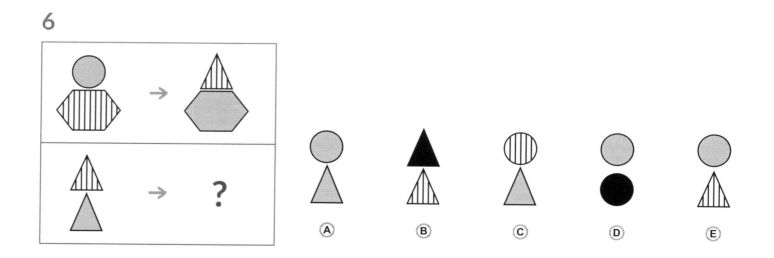

7

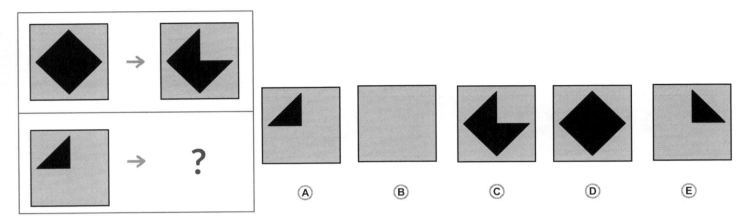

8

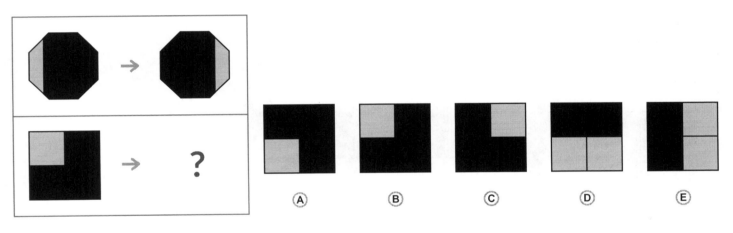

9

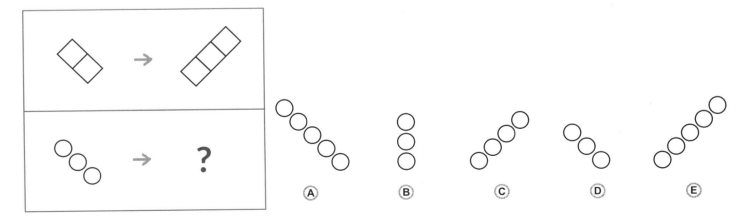

73

10

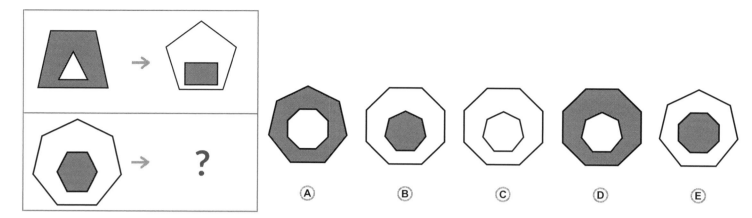

11

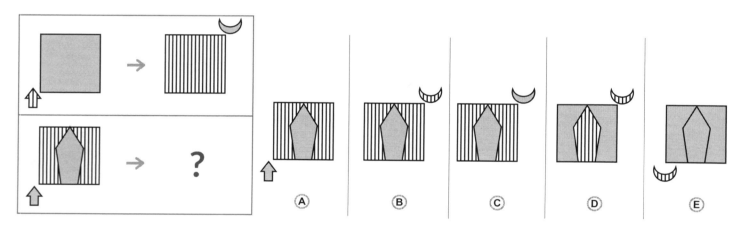

12

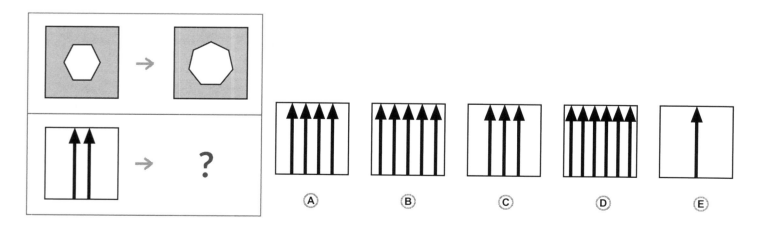

13

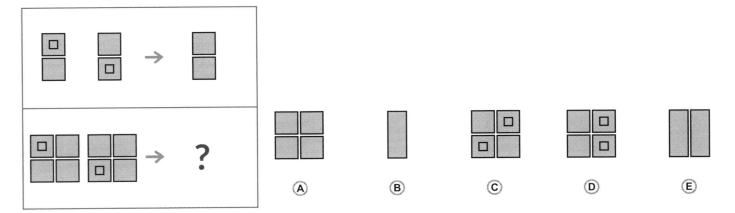

14

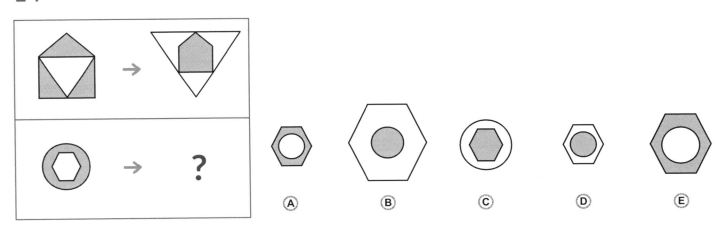

15

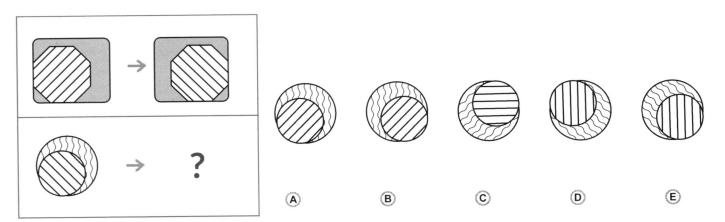

16

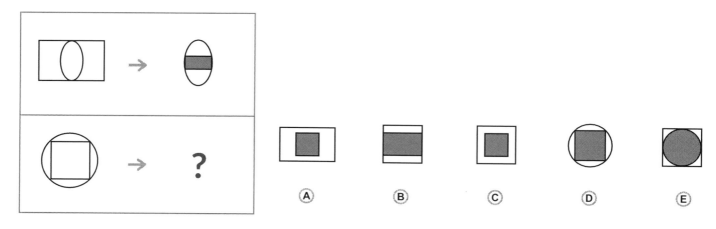

17

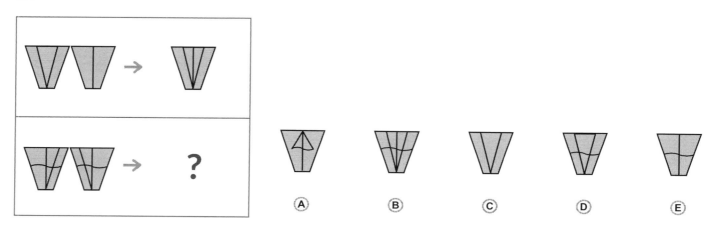

18

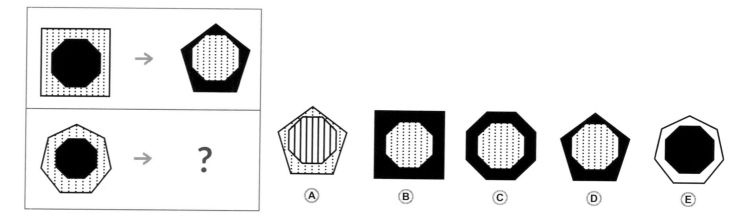

PAPER FOLDING   Directions: The top row of pictures shows a sheet of paper. The paper was folded, then something was cut out. Which picture in the bottom row shows how the paper would look after it's unfolded?

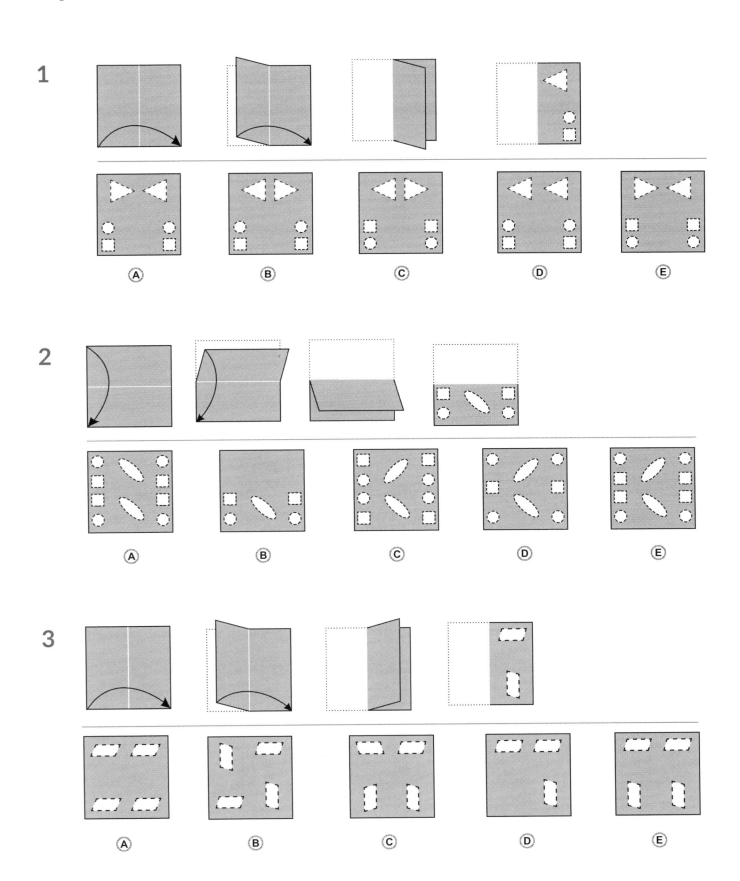

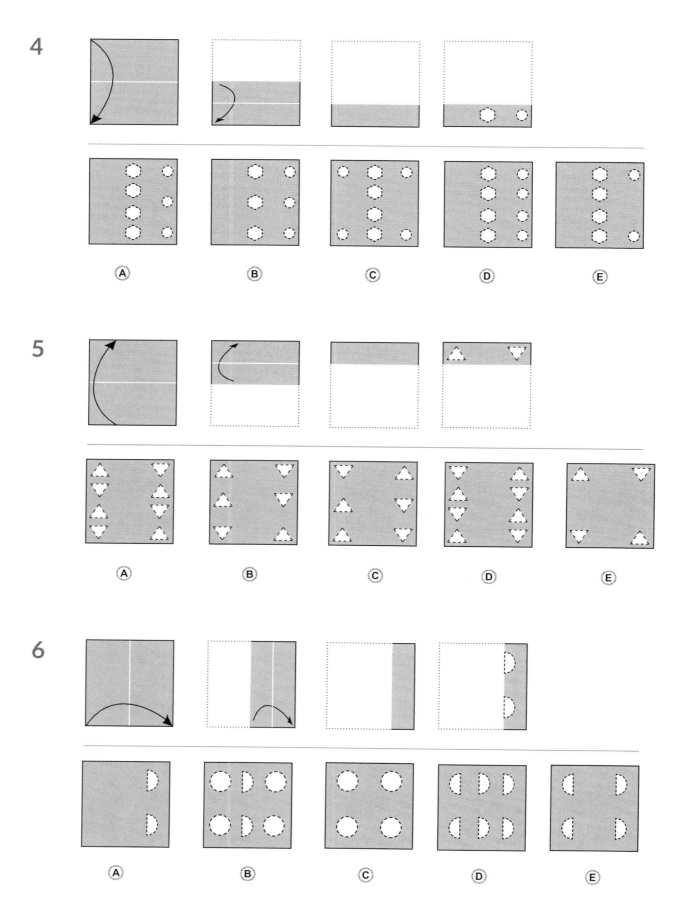

7

8

9

10

A   B   C   D   E

11

A   B   C   D   E

12

A   B   C   D   E

13

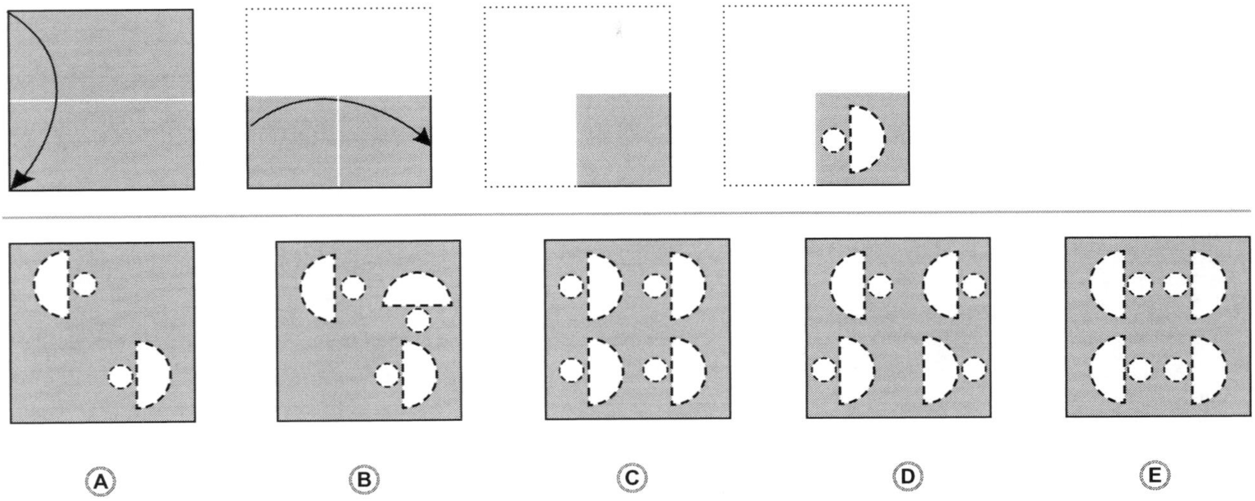

A   B   C   D   E

14

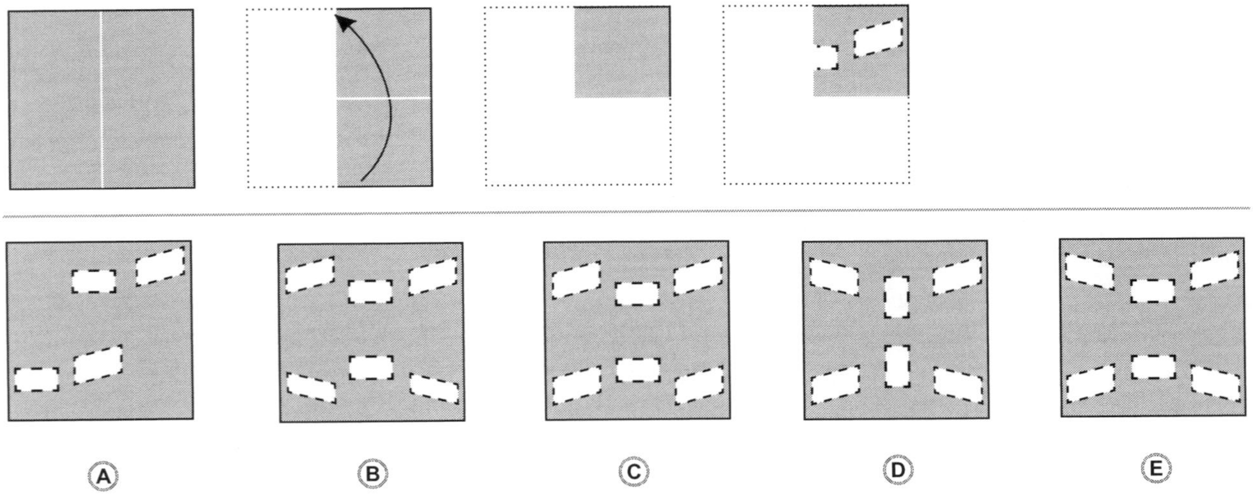

A   B   C   D   E

15

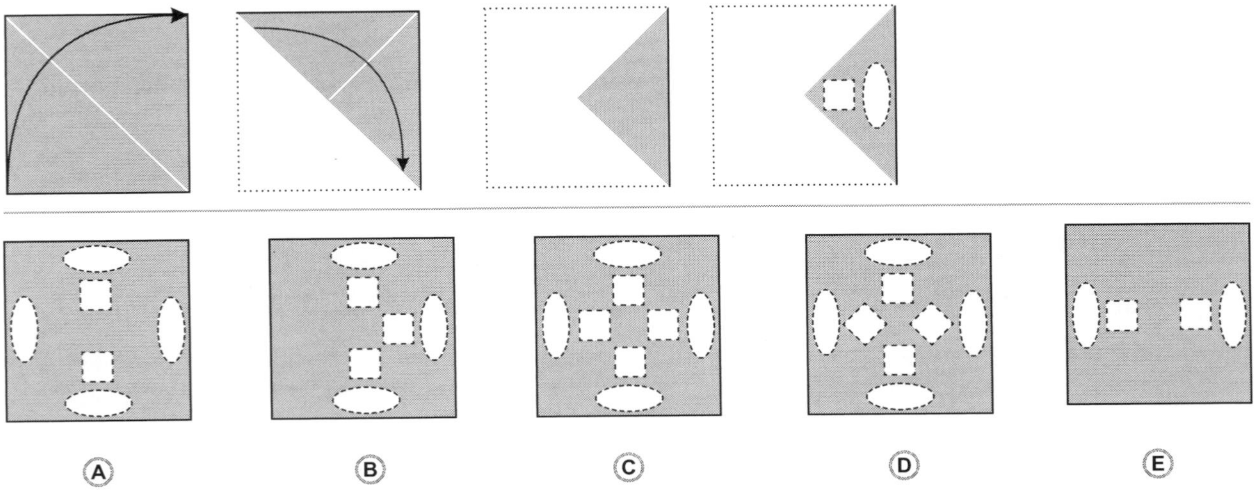

A   B   C   D   E

Directions: Which number would go in place of the question mark so that both of sides of the equal sign (point to the equal sign) have the same amount?

1 $56 = 48 + \boxed{?}$

(A) 18   (B) 8   (C) 48   (D) 104   (E) 12

2 $34 = 66 - \boxed{?}$

(A) 100   (B) 12   (C) 22   (D) 18   (E) 32

3 $55 / \boxed{?} = 5$

(A) 10   (B) 50   (C) 60   (D) 11   (E) 5

4 $8 \times \boxed{?} = 32$

(A) 4   (B) 24   (C) 40   (D) 6   (E) 3

5 $34 + 28 = 71 - \boxed{?}$

(A) 62   (B) 9   (C) 65   (D) 19   (E) 29

6

$$49 - 37 = 68 - \boxed{?}$$

(A) 12   (B) 46   (C) 36   (D) 18   (E) 56

7

$$34 + 7 = 44 - \boxed{?}$$

(A) 17   (B) 12   (C) 2   (D) 3   (E) 41

8

$$40 = \boxed{?} \times 5$$

(A) 7   (B) 5   (C) 8   (D) 9   (E) 35

9

$$\boxed{?} = \blacklozenge + 27 + 3$$
$$\blacklozenge = 7$$

(A) 2   (B) 37   (C) 65   (D) 59   (E) 2

10

$$\boxed{?} = \blacklozenge + 39 - 18$$
$$\blacklozenge = 22$$

(A) 79   (B) 21   (C) 14   (D) 43   (E) 22

11

$$42 \quad + \quad 19 \quad = \quad 63 \quad - \quad \boxed{?}$$

(A) 61   (B) 12   (C) 2   (D) 17   (E) 40

12

$$64 \quad = \quad 55 \quad - \quad 37 \quad + \quad \boxed{?}$$

(A) 46   (B) 28   (C) 18   (D) 36   (E) 56

13

$$\boxed{?} \quad = \quad \blacklozenge \quad + \quad 52$$
$$\blacklozenge \quad = \quad 18$$

(A) 70   (B) 60   (C) 80   (D) 34   (E) 18

14

$$\boxed{?} \quad = \quad \blacklozenge \quad \times \quad 6$$
$$\blacklozenge \quad = \quad 8$$

(A) 2   (B) 14   (C) 48   (D) 40   (E) 56

15

$$\boxed{?} \quad = \quad \blacklozenge \quad / \quad 4$$
$$\blacklozenge \quad = \quad 28$$

(A) 14   (B) 7   (C) 24   (D) 6   (E) 32

16

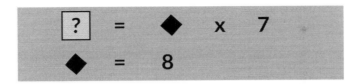

$? = \blacklozenge \times 7$

$\blacklozenge = 8$

(A) 15   (B) 1   (C) 56   (D) 64   (E) 42

17

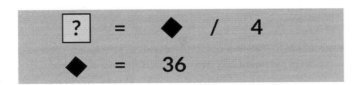

$? = \blacklozenge / 4$

$\blacklozenge = 36$

(A) 8   (B) 32   (C) 40   (D) 7   (E) 9

18

$? = \blacklozenge + 34 - 25$

$\blacklozenge = 61$

(A) 95   (B) 5   (C) 37   (D) 70   (E) 52

19

$? = \blacklozenge + 27 + 34$

$\blacklozenge = 18$

(A) 79   (B) 77   (C) 11   (D) 61   (E) 69

20

$? = \blacklozenge - 48 - 12$

$\blacklozenge = 65$

(A) 36   (B) 101   (C) 29   (D) 15   (E) 5

Directions: Which answer choice would complete the pattern?

1

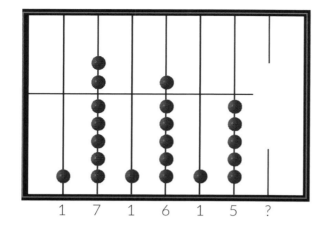

1   7   1   6   1   5   ?

3	4	1	6	8
(A)	(B)	(C)	(D)	(E)

2

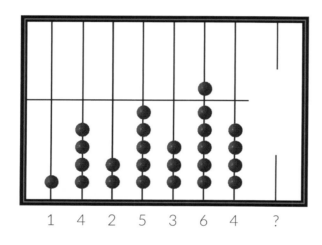

1   4   2   5   3   6   4   ?

5	0	1	7	8
(A)	(B)	(C)	(D)	(E)

3

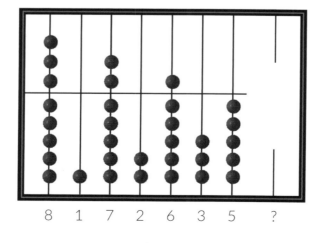

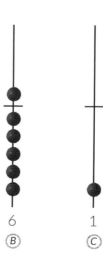

8   1   7   2   6   3   5   ?

5	6	1	7	4
(A)	(B)	(C)	(D)	(E)

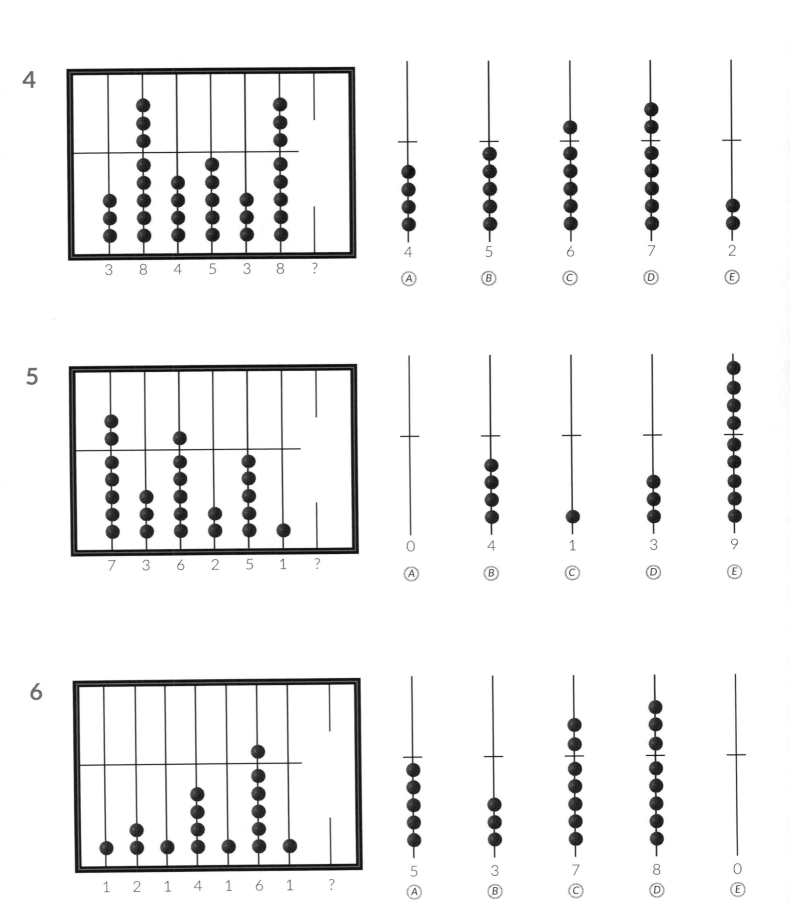

1   38   40   42   44   46   48   ?

(A) 50   (B) 52   (C) 51   (D) 24   (E) 84

2   19   33   47   61   75   89   ?

(A) 99   (B) 100   (C) 101   (D) 102   (E) 103

3   19   17   16   14   13   11   ?

(A) 8   (B) 9   (C) 10   (D) 12   (E) 2

4   0   2   0   3   0   4   ?

(A) 5   (B) 4   (C) 0   (D) 3   (E) 6

5   89   77   65   53   41   29   ?

(A) 11   (B) 12   (C) 15   (D) 16   (E) 17

6   41   41   42   42   43   43   ?

(A) 44   (B) 45   (C) 43   (D) 53   (E) 40

7 64.5   64.0   63.5   63.0   62.5   62.0   ?

    Ⓐ 60.51   Ⓑ 62.15   Ⓒ 62.5   Ⓓ 61.5   Ⓔ 60.5

8 37   38   43   44   49   50   ?

    Ⓐ 51   Ⓑ 54   Ⓒ 55   Ⓓ 56   Ⓔ 57

9 20   19   18   16   15   14   ?

    Ⓐ 13   Ⓑ 12   Ⓒ 11   Ⓓ 10   Ⓔ 2

10 34.8   32.8   30.8   28.8   26.8   24.8   ?

    Ⓐ 24   Ⓑ 20   Ⓒ 22   Ⓓ 20.8   Ⓔ 22.8

11 88   78   75   65   62   52   ?

    Ⓐ 22   Ⓑ 32   Ⓒ 39   Ⓓ 49   Ⓔ 42

12 39   37   38   36   37   35   ?

    Ⓐ 36   Ⓑ 37   Ⓒ 35   Ⓓ 34   Ⓔ 30

NUMBER ANALOGIES

Directions: Look at the first set of numbers. It goes together in some way. Look at the second set of numbers. It goes together in some way. Both of these sets must go together in the same way. Look at the third set where there is a question mark. What number should go here so that all three sets of numbers go together in the same way?

1

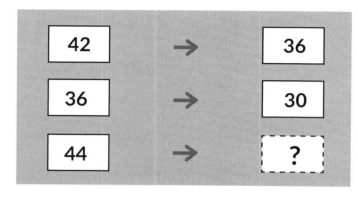

Ⓐ 42   Ⓑ 36   Ⓒ 16   Ⓓ 50   Ⓔ 38

2

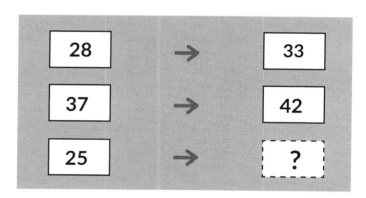

Ⓐ 9   Ⓑ 7   Ⓒ 30   Ⓓ 20   Ⓔ 5

3

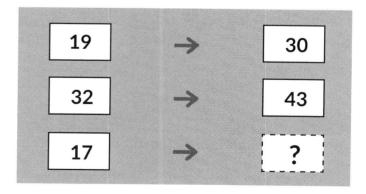

Ⓐ 44   Ⓑ 29   Ⓒ 16   Ⓓ 28   Ⓔ 54

4

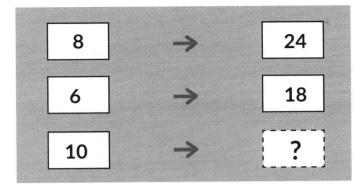

(A) 30   (B) 13   (C) 7   (D) 21   (E) 24

5

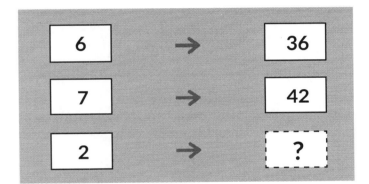

(A) 18   (B) 14   (C) 8   (D) 12   (E) 6

6

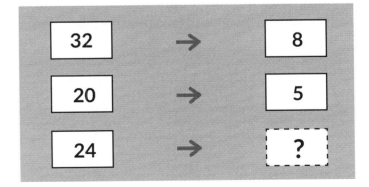

(A) 28   (B) 6   (C) 8   (D) 4   (E) 20

7   [33 → 42]   [11 → 20]   [52 → ?]

(A) 59   (B) 60   (C) 61   (D) 43   (E) 29

8   [32 → 28]   [53 → 49]   [41 → ?]

(A) 45   (B) 27   (C) 29   (D) 37   (E) 38

9   [46 → 39]   [32 → 25]   [24 → ?]

(A) 7   (B) 17   (C) 18   (D) 31   (E) 8

10   [5 → 10]   [15 → 20]   [29 → ?]

(A) 21   (B) 30   (C) 35   (D) 24   (E) 34

11   [21 → 15]   [48 → 42]   [10 → ?]

(A) 12   (B) 16   (C) 4   (D) 8   (E) 6

12   [41 → 29]   [38 → 26]   [24 → ?]

(A) 26   (B) 12   (C) 2   (D) 14   (E) 4

13 [29 → 37]   [41 → 49]   [34 → ?]

    Ⓐ 52   Ⓑ 26   Ⓒ 42   Ⓓ 18   Ⓔ 36

14 [18 → 9]   [22 → 11]   [6 → ?]

    Ⓐ 3   Ⓑ 2   Ⓒ 4   Ⓓ 6   Ⓔ 8

15 [10 → 1]   [50 → 5]   [60 → ?]

    Ⓐ 70   Ⓑ 9   Ⓒ 10   Ⓓ 11   Ⓔ 6

16 [7 → 28]   [10 → 40]   [9 → ?]

    Ⓐ 13   Ⓑ 5   Ⓒ 8   Ⓓ 36   Ⓔ 4

17 [5 → 1]   [30 → 6]   [20 → ?]

    Ⓐ 24   Ⓑ 6   Ⓒ 5   Ⓓ 4   Ⓔ 16

18 [18 → 3]   [24 → 4]   [42 → ?]

    Ⓐ 6   Ⓑ 7   Ⓒ 8   Ⓓ 5   Ⓔ 48

ANSWER KEY FOR PRACTICE TEST 1

- At the end of each section of questions, total the number of questions your child correctly answered.
- This will provide a general overview of strengths/challenges according to COGAT® question type.

Verbal Classification, Practice Test 1

1. E.
2. C. vegetables
3. D. colors
4. B. parts of arm
5. B. jewelry
6. D. months
7. B. things that provide light
8. A. living things that are pretend
9. A. parts of a building
10. C. words having to do with things being the same
11. B. parts of a book
12. A. plants
13. C. things people wear
14. B. words having to do with things getting larger
15. D. things that are white
16. E. things that travel on water
17. D. hot liquids
18. B. fruit (note it's not "words that start with the letter 'P'" because there are two choices that start with "P")
19. E. having to do with the highest part of something
20. D. adjectives that describe things that are not common

Verbal Classification Questions Answered Correctly: _____ out of 20

Verbal Analogies, Practice Test 1

1. E.
2. B. Laces fasten shoes. A zipper fastens a jacket. (fasten = to attach or join)
3. B. Texas is a state. Africa is a continent.
4. C. A scale is used to measure weight. A thermometer is used to measure temperature.
5. D. Grapes grow on a vine. Pears grow on a tree.
6. C. A person's hand is like an animal's paw. A person's fingernail is like an animal's claw.
7. D. A boulder is a very large rock. A mountain is a very large hill. (Larger version > smaller version)
8. A. A snake and a lizard are both reptiles. A parrot and a chicken are both birds.
9. E. A minute is used to measure time. An inch is used to measure length.
10. D. Ears are a body part used for the sense of hearing. The tongue is a body part used for the sense of taste.
11. B. A faster, motorized version of a canoe (a type of boat) is a speedboat. A faster, motorized version of a wagon (a vehicle made to transport things) is a truck.
12. C. A school is lead by a principal. A ship is lead by a captain.
13. A. A television runs on/is powered by electricity. A flashlight runs on/is powered by batteries.
14. D. Homophones (words that sound alike but are spelled differently and have a different meaning).
15. D. A slice is part of a loaf. A petal is part of a flower. Or, a group of slices makes up a loaf. A group of petals makes up a flower.
16. A. You would find a monkey in a jungle. You would find a sink in a bathroom.
17. B. Something that is extremely cool is frigid. Something that is extremely large is enormous.
18. C. Something very good is excellent. Something very funny is hilarious.
19. E. A director directs actors. A conductor directs musicians.
20. D. A pigeon is one of a group of birds found in a flock. An apple is one of a group of apples found in a bushel.
21. A. Antonyms (opposites).
22. B. A detective carries out investigations for their job. A scientist carries out experiments for their job.

Verbal Analogies Questions Answered Correctly: _____ out of 22

Sentence Completion, Practice Test 1

1. C. swift = fast
2. E. distant = far away
3. A. rate = the number of times something happens during an amount of time / the speed that something happens during an amount of time
4. B. scatter = to throw in different, random directions
5. C. approach = to get closer to something
6. B. consider = to think carefully about something
7. B. resident = someone who lives somewhere (for a longer amount of time)
8. C. essential = necessary / very important
9. A. rely = to depend on/to count on
10. B. observe = to notice something (something that is often important)
11. B. reveal = to make information known to others (information that was not known before)
12. E. mature = being similar to an adult (here, in how you behave and your level of responsibility)
13. E. proceed = to continue or to move forward with
14. D. recover = to get back to normal health after being injured or being sick
15. B. here, make sure your child pays attention to the word "despite"
16. C. stable = in good condition & not easily moved
17. A. prevent = to keep something from happening
18. D. harsh = severe or very difficult
19. E. ancient = from the very distant past
20. A. reduce = to make less
21. B. descend = to go down
22. D. distract = to take attention away from something or someone
23. B. peculiar = strange
24. E. custom = made for specifically for someone

Sentence Completion Questions Answered Correctly: _____ out of 24

Figure Classification, Practice Test 1

1. E.   2. D. triangles
3. B. divided into 3 equal parts
4. C. group of 3 shapes
5. A. octagon in middle
6. D. inside square are 3 sections; 1 has straight vertical lines; 2 have thin wavy lines
7. C. inside circle sections are a star & heart that are directly next to each other
8. E. 3 arrows point down & 1 points up
9. D. the bottom shape has rotated 90 degrees counterclockwise (to the left)
10. B. the line on the "V" is in the middle of the "V"
11. B. arrows alternate color gray/white
12. C. as the design rotates, the black "point" remains at the same place on the "L" shape
13. D. the shape is divided into quarters (fourths) and one-quarter (1/4) of it has solid horizontal lines
14. C. the heart & the star are different colors
15. E. one of the three shapes has: black, dotted lines, or solid horizontal lines
16. D. there are 3 different figures with different color/design inside: gray, white, or vertical lines (A & E are not correct - the "U" is upside down)
17. A. shape is cut in half from lower left to upper right
18. B. as shape rotates, the side that's gray & the side that's white remains the same

Figure Classification Questions Answered Correctly: _____ out of 18

Figure Analogies, Practice Test 1

1. D.
2. A. two arrows are removed
3. D. rotates clockwise 90 degrees
4. E. rotates clockwise 90 degrees (like #3, but a different design)
5. A. in the box with 4 sections, the top left shape & bottom right shape switch position (on top, it's the triangle and square; on the bottom & in the answer it's the trapezoid & hexagon)
6. B. smaller shapes outside the larger gray shape move inside the larger gray shape
7. C. white becomes gray & gray becomes white
8. C. outer shape & inner shape switch positions (also, inner shape becomes larger, outer shape becomes smaller)
9. A. group of white shapes align horizontally, largest to smallest, and turn gray
10. D. outer shape becomes inner shape (and gets smaller), smaller shape in the very middle becomes outer shape (and gets bigger), middle shape becomes larger also
11. D. number of arrow points = number of shape sides
12. C. shape designs change like this: gray becomes black, wavy lines become gray, black becomes wavy lines -or- the bottom shape moves to the top
13. E. colors change like this: black stays the same, white becomes gray, gray becomes white
14. B. smaller shape that was inside larger shape is now by itself and larger
15. A. top left & bottom right shapes switch position; bottom left & top right switch position
16. A. sections of shape switch colors like this: black becomes gray, dotted lines become black
17. E. one arrow is added & the arrow group has rotated 90 degrees clockwise
18. B. the bottom shape gets bigger; the top shape and the middle shape move inside the bottom shape; the top shape also gets bigger; the middle shape (the heart) rotates 90 degrees clockwise
19. D. two hearts appear in the group of shapes from the left box

Figure Analogies Questions Answered Correctly: _____ out of 19

Paper Folding, Practice Test 1

1. D   2. B   3. A   4. C   5. E   6. A   7. E   8. B   9. E   10. E   11. C   12. D   13. A   14. E   15. B   16. B   17. D

Paper Folding Questions Answered Correctly: _____ out of 17

Number Puzzles, Practice Test 1

1. D   2. B   3. B   4. E   5. D   6. A   7. E   8. D   9. A   10. B   11. B   12. C   13. D   14. C   15. E   16. A   17. E

Number Puzzles Answered Correctly: _____ out of 17

Number Series, Practice Test 1

1. B.   2. C.   3. C. 3-4-5-6   4. D. rods 1, 3, 5 increase by 1; rods 2, 4, 6 = 6
5. A. rods 1, 3, 5 incr. by 1; rods 2, 4, 6 incr. by 1   6. D. 5-2-4-1
7. A. rods 1, 3, 5 decrease by 1; rods 2, 4, 6 decr. by 1   8. C. 3-1-1   9. C. +3
10. D. +1, +2, +1, +2, etc.   11. A. -1, -2, -1, -2, etc.   12. D. +2, +3, +2, +3, etc.
13. E. +2, -3, +2, -3, etc.   14. E. +2, +0, +2, +0   15. C. +2.0 (or, +2)   16. A. +0.02
17. B. -1, -1, -2, -1, -1, -2   18. C. +7   19. D. +1.1

Number Series Answered Correctly: _____ out of 19

Number Analogies, Practice Test 1

1. D. +1   2. C. x2   3. A. +3   4. E. x4   5. B. -5   6. D. ÷3   7. A. ÷10
8. C. +9   9. E. ÷2   10. D. -8   11. B. -6   12. B. +7   13. A. -8   14. E. x6
15. C. -9   16. D. ÷4   17. C. -7   18. B. ÷3

Number Analogies Answered Correctly: _____ out of 18

ANSWER KEY FOR PRACTICE TEST 2

Verbal Classification, Practice Test 2

1. D. types of fish   2. B. sports   3. A. school supplies
4. C. used to heat food   5. C. instruments
6. D. wind instruments (compared to question #5 this question is more challenging as these are a specific kind of instrument)
7. A. countries   8. B. adjectives that describe having strength   9. A. senses
10. B. 3-D shapes   11. C. nationalities   12. C. landforms   13. C. mammals
14. A. cold weather clothing   15. B. travel on land   16. D. places that are meant for walking
17. B. things that are the color black/are very dark   18. E. bodies of water
19. B. things having to do with 2 of something   20. E. things having to do with the end

Verbal Classification Questions Answered Correctly: _____ out of 20

Verbal Analogies, Practice Test 2

1. B. Antonyms (opposites)
2. D. A brush is a tool a painter uses to do their job. A hammer is a tool a carpenter uses to do their job.
3. D. A bouquet is made from a group of flowers put together. A book is made from pages put together.
4. E. Months make up a year. Players make up a team.
5. C. Bees produce a food people eat which is honey. Chickens produce a food people eat which is eggs.
6. C. A shovel is used to dig things. A towel is used to dry things.
7. B. Action > Version of this action with movement added (swimming when in water; walking when on ground)
8. C. Adjective > Extreme version of this adjective
9. B. A baseball is used with a bat, and it is hit by a bat. A nail is used with a hammer, and it is hit by a hammer.
10. D. A necklace is a type of jewelry. A sofa is a type of furniture.
11. A. A pencil is used to sketch. A brush is used to paint.
12. B. A carpenter builds things. A mechanic repairs things.
13. E. You kick a ball. You climb a ladder.
14. B. States make up a country. Trees make up a forest.
15. C. Synonyms (words with similar meanings).
16. D. A car is a type of vehicle. A bee is a type of animal.
17. A. Used together. A scarf and a jacket are used together by a person as clothing. A sheet and a pillow are used together on a bed for sleeping.
18. E. Antonyms (opposites)
19. C. A virus causes sickness. Rain causes floods.

Verbal Analogies Questions Answered Correctly: _____ out of 19

Sentence Completion Practice Test 2

1. B. limit = to keep something from being larger
2. E. reverse = to go in the opposite direction
3. E. additional = more
4. D. envy = to want a thing someone else has
5. A. attract = to cause someone to like something or to be interested in something
6. B. recall = to remember
7. D. manufacture = to make something using machines
8. A. primary = main
9. D. advantage = something that gives you a better chance of success
10. B. intend = to plan
11. B. indicates = shows
12. A. suitable = right for a certain purpose or situation
13. A. eager = very interested in/excited about something
14. B. permit = a document that shows someone is allowed to do something or to have something
15. E. gradual = happening slowly
16. C. tragic = very sad, very bad
17. C. persuade = to make someone do or believe something by asking them or giving them reasons
18. B. previous = happening before
19. A. available = able/ready to be used
20. B. vast = very large, spread out, and covering a lot of area

Sentence Completion Questions Answered Correctly: _____ out of 20

Figure Classification, Practice Test 2

1. D. triangles facing same direction
2. B. shapes filled with dots
3. A. triangles
4. D. as shape group rotates, gray circle remains at same spot on the arrows
5. C. inside circle, there are 2 pairs of the same shape; these pairs are across from each other
6. E. there are: 2 white squares, 1 square with dots, 1 square with a circle inside
7. B. tic-tac-toe with the white triangles
8. E. the pentagon & arrow are across from each other inside the circle sections
9. D. inside square's sections, the oval & triangle are next to each other & there is a heart
10. B. pentagon in the middle
11. A. the white shape is a smaller version of the large shape that's divided; the large shape has a white section & a section with horizontal lines
12. C. each shape group has a: heart, triangle, octagon
13. E. inside each shape are 3 lines that cross each other
14. C. each shape group has exactly 1 gray circle
15. C. inside shape has 1 more side than outer shape
16. B. rectangles are divided into equal parts
17. B. 7-sided shapes
18. B. shapes alternate: gray / vertical lines

Figure Classification Questions Answered Correctly: _____ out of 18

Figure Analogies, Practice Test 2

1. D. shape rotates 180 degrees & another identical shape is added
2. E. design of inner & outer shape switch
3. A. a rectangle is added between the 2 original rectangles
4. C. white shape in the original figure appears alone & rotates 90 degrees counterclockwise
5. E. small black shape gets bigger; inside the larger black shape are 2 versions of the original gray shape; these 2 gray shapes have gotten smaller; the larger of the 2 is on the bottom
6. E. the gray circle becomes a triangle filled with vertical lines & vice versa; the bottom shape changes from being filled with vertical lines to being gray and vice versa
7. B. across the row, there is 1 less section of the diamond
8. C. shape flips/becomes mirror image
9. C. shape group flips/becomes mirror image and 1 more shape is added
10. D. outer shape has 1 more side than inner shape & colors have switched
11. D. in the square and in the smaller shape, gray changes to vertical lines & vice versa; the arrow in the lower left corner becomes a crescent and moves to the upper right corner
12. C. one more is added: on top there's a shape where 1 more side has been added; on the bottom one more arrow has been added
13. A. one of the shape groups has been removed & there are no smaller squares inside this shape group
14. B. the smaller white shape in the middle gets bigger & becomes the outer shape; the larger gray shape gets smaller and moves inside
15. B. the smaller shape inside moves to the opposite side & the diagonal lines switch the direction they are pointing
16. E. the larger outer shape moves inside the center shape and becomes gray
17. B. the second boxes (the right boxes) have the combination of lines that appear in the middle of the trapezoids
18. C. the middle shape (an octagon) switches from black to being filled with dots; the outer shape becomes a shape with one more side

Figure Analogies Questions Answered Correctly: _____ out of 18

Paper Folding, Practice Test 2

1. A	2. E	3. C	4. D	5. A	6. C	7. B	8. E
9. B	10. C	11. B	12. D	13. E	14. E	15. C	

Paper Folding Questions Answered Correctly: _____ out of 15

Number Puzzles, Practice Test 2

1. B	2. E	3. D	4. A	5. B	6. E	7. D	8. C
9. B	10. D	11. C	12. A	13. A	14. C	15. B	16. C
17. E	18. D	19. A	20. E				

Number Puzzles Questions Answered Correctly: _____ out of 20

Number Series - Abacus, Practice Test 2

1. C. rods 1, 3, 5 = 1; rods 2, 4, 6 decr. by 1
2. D. rods 1, 3, 5, 7 incr. by 1; rods 2,4,6 incr. by 1
3. E. rods 1, 3, 5, 7 decr. 1; rods 2, 4, 6 incr. by 1
4. A. 3-8-4-5
5. B. rods 1, 3, 5, 7 decr. 1; rods 2, 4, 6 decr. by 1
6. D. rods 1, 3, 5 = 1; rods 2,4,6 incr. by 2

Number Series - Text, Practice Test 2

1. A. +2   2. E. +14   3. C. -2, -1, -2, -1, etc.
4. C. in places 1,3,5 there's a "0"; in places 2,4,6 you add +1
5. E. -12
6. A. +0, +1, +0, +1, +0 -OR- the numbers repeat and increase by 1
7. D. -0.5
8. C. +1, +5, +1, +5, +1   9. B. -1, -1, -2, -1, -1   10. E. -2.0 (or, -2)
11. D. -10, -3, -10, -3, etc.   12. A. -2, +1, -2, +1, etc.

Number Series Questions Answered Correctly: _____ out of 18

Number Analogies, p. 85, Practice Test 2

1. E. -6   2. C. +5   3. D. +11   4. A. x3   5. D. x6
6. B. ÷4   7. C. +9   8. D. -4   9. B. -7   10. E. +5
11. C. -6   12. B. -12   13. C. +8   14. A. ÷2   15. E. ÷10
16. D. x4   17. D. ÷5   18. B. ÷6

Number Analogies Questions Answered Correctly: _____ out of 18

Made in the USA
Middletown, DE
01 February 2024

48868960R00057